D1168844

Caring for Words
in a Culture of Lies

Caring for Words
in a Culture of Lies

MARILYN CHANDLER McENTYRE

*This book originated as the
2004 Stone Lectures at
Princeton Theological Seminary*

William B. Eerdmans Publishing Company

Grand Rapids, Michigan / Cambridge, U.K.

© 2009 Marilyn Chandler McEntyre

All rights reserved

Published 2009 by

Wm. B. Eerdmans Publishing Co.

2140 Oak Industrial Drive N.E., Grand Rapids, Michigan 49505 /
P.O. Box 163, Cambridge CB3 9PU U.K.

Printed in the United States of America

14 13 12 11 10   7 6 5 4 3 2

Library of Congress Cataloging-in-Publication Data

McEntyre, Marilyn Chandler, 1949-
Caring for words in a culture of lies / Marilyn Chandler McEntyre.
p.   cm.
Includes bibliographical references.
ISBN 978-0-8028-4864-2 (alk. paper)
1. Truthfulness and falsehood — Religious aspects —
Christianity. 2. Language and languages — Religious aspects —
Christianity. I. Title.

BV4647.T7M34   2009
241′.673 — dc22

2009006926

www.eerdmans.com

In loving memory of

Mary and LeGare Chandler
and
Jack and Effie Chandler

who taught me to speak
and to listen
and to appreciate the punch line

Contents

CONTENTS

A Word of Thanks

I am grateful to Princeton Theological Seminary for offering me the privilege of delivering the Stone Lectures in 2004 that became the core of this book, and to William B. Eerdmans and Mary Hietbrink for their help in bringing it to its present form.

I am particularly grateful to George and Deborah Hunsinger, both professors at Princeton Seminary, for their friendship and encouragement in this endeavor.

I am grateful to my colleagues in the English and Modern Language Departments at Westmont College for the depth and fidelity I have witnessed in their care for language and story. Over the past twelve years I have learned much from each of them.

I am grateful to more students than I can name here who, over thirty years of teaching, have asked questions and crafted sentences that taught me something new about how to use words and listen to them. You know who you are. Thank you.

I am grateful to the friends who have recited poems or read aloud or quoted lines they loved or poked holes in propaganda or sustained nourishing conversation into the wee hours.

I am grateful to my brother, David, who speaks truth, clearly, to power.

I am grateful to each of our six children and their sweet spouses and significant others for the ways their words warm my heart. I hope to stay in conversation with you as long as language is given to me.

I am grateful for the chance to watch five little boys make their way into speech and song. Stephen, Matthew, Thomas, Christopher, and Benjamin, may you learn many words and use them with wit and grace.

And I am deeply grateful, more than words can express, for John. The conversation we share sustains me in the darkest times, keeps me accountable, and makes every day a gift.

An Introductory Word to Readers

Gentle Readers,

The sense of urgency that fueled these reflections on caring for words has grown over years of teaching literature, writing, listening to lectures, sermons, and State of the Union addresses, and seeking ways to impart to the young "the joy of a graceful sentence." Although the opening chapter is rather darkly diagnostic, I hope you will press on to the remaining chapters, which are meant to offer encouragement. There are gracious and inventive ways to enjoy words and to reclaim them as instruments of love, healing, and peace. All of us who speak, read, write, and listen to each other have opportunities to do that and to foster the kinds of community that come from shared stories and surprising sentences.

Because these chapters began as talks given as the Stone Lectures at Princeton Theological Seminary, many of my observations are directed specifically to people of faith who may share my concerns about how to read

Scripture and how to take responsibility for the stories Christians hold in trust as heirs of that tradition. I hope, though, that any of you who care about language and story, whether because of your own faith traditions or because of your love for conversation, or for literature, or for children just learning to speak, will find here an invitation to reflect and to act in protection of the gift of language that binds us into human community.

If you've ever loved and learned a poem by heart, or underlined sentences just because they were beautiful, or labored over a speech about something that mattered, I know we share the concerns and the pleasures of stewards who recognize that we hold a great treasure in trust. It is my hope that a sentence here and there will start a conversation or encourage some of you to speak the truth that is in you, to find a sentence that suffices in a hard time, or simply to listen into the silences where the best words begin.

Marilyn Chandler McEntyre

Why Worry about Words?

I was talking recently about stewardship of resources with a young man who is hoping to make a career in environmental law. We considered the fate of water, soil, animal and plant species, and food systems. In the wake of that invigorating conversation, I found myself musing on the similar problems that beset another precious shared resource: words. Like any other life-sustaining resource, language can be depleted, polluted, contaminated, eroded, and filled with artificial stimulants. Like any other resource, it needs the protection of those who recognize its value and commit themselves to good stewardship.

In these essays I'd like to reflect on what it might mean to be good stewards of language — what it might mean to retrieve words from the kinds of misuse, abuse, and distortion to which they've been subjected of late, and to reinvigorate them for use as bearers of truth and as instruments of love.

Caring for language is a moral issue. Caring for one

another is not entirely separable from caring for words. Words are entrusted to us as equipment for our life together, to help us survive, guide, and nourish one another. We need to take the metaphor of nourishment seriously in choosing what we "feed on" in our hearts, and in seeking to make our conversation with each other life-giving. A large, almost sacramental sense of the import and efficacy of words can be found in early English usage, where *conversation* appears to have been a term that included and implied much more than it does now: to converse was to foster community, to commune with, to dwell in a place with others. Conversation was understood to be a life-sustaining practice, a blessing, and a craft to be cultivated for the common good. A quaint poem by Edward Taylor offers some sense of this larger notion of conversation: developing the image of the self as God's "spinning wheel," Taylor prays, "and make my Soule thy holy Spoole to bee. My conversation make to be thy Reele."[1] The business of gently guiding rough strands pulled from the gathered wool into grooves where they may become fine thread suggests a rich idea of conversation as right, skillful, careful, economical use of what God and nature have provided for our use and protection.

1. Edward Taylor, "Huswifery," in *The Poems of Edward Taylor*, ed. Donald E. Stanford (Chapel Hill: University of North Carolina Press, 1989), p. 343.

To call upon another analogy, if language is to retain its power to nourish and sustain our common life, we have to care for it in something like the way good farmers care for the life of the soil, knowing nothing worth eating can be grown in soil that has been used up, overfertilized, or exposed to too many toxic chemicals. The comparison, I believe, is pertinent, timely, and precise — and urgent.

Not that the state of language is a matter for despair: there is much to celebrate in our verbal environment. Poets are featured weekly on public radio; dozens of versions of the English Bible are in print; Garrison Keillor is still telling stories and "pretty good jokes"; bilingual poets are stretching and enriching public discourse; Billy Collins and Toni Morrison are very likely at their keyboards even as we speak. Libraries offer programs for preschoolers, bookstores still stock Shakespeare, and every summer there's a theater festival somewhere nearby. PBS and Pacifica Radio still feature articulate analysts. The sheer availability of words — written, spoken, and sung — is historically unprecedented.

Stewardship of such riches is a weighty responsibility, perhaps never more so than now, because as venues for the spoken and written word abound, so do the varieties of language abuse: propaganda, imprecision, clichés, and cant. Warnings about the consequences of language abuse have been issued before. George Orwell in 1946 and George Steiner in 1959 lamented the way that language, co-opted and twisted to serve corporate, commercial, and political agendas, could lose its resiliency, utility, and beauty. Their arguments are still widely cited. Orwell, for instance, makes this claim:

> [The English language] becomes ugly and inaccurate because our thoughts are foolish, but the slovenliness of our language makes it easier for us to have foolish thoughts. The point is that the process is reversible. Modern English, especially written English, is full of bad habits which spread by imitation and which can be avoided if one is willing to take the necessary trouble. If one gets rid of these habits, one can think more clearly, and to think clearly is a necessary first step toward political regeneration: so that the fight against bad English is not frivolous and is not the exclusive concern of professional writers.[2]

This description, like Orwell's ominous vision of "newspeak" in *1984*, may have an unsettling ring of familiarity. In a similar vein, but rather more bleakly, George Steiner reflects on what actually happened to the German language under the Third Reich:

2. George Orwell, "Politics and the English Language," in *George Orwell: A Collection of Essays* (New York: Harcourt, 1946; Harvest edition, 1981), p. 157.

4

> The language was infected not only with ... great besti-
> alities. It was called upon to enforce innumerable false-
> hoods, to persuade the Germans that the war was just
> and everywhere victorious. As defeat closed in ... the
> lies thickened to a constant snowdrift. ...

He goes on to comment,

> Languages have great reserves of life. They can absorb
> masses of hysteria, illiteracy, and cheapness. ... But
> there comes a breaking point. Use a language to con-
> ceive, organize, and justify Belsen; use it to make out
> specifications for gas ovens; use it to dehumanize man
> during twelve years of calculated bestiality. Something
> will happen to it. ... Something of the lies and sadism
> will settle in the marrow of the language. Imperceptibly
> at first, like the poisons of radiation sifting silently into
> the bone. But the cancer will begin, and the deep-set
> destruction. The language will no longer grow and
> freshen. It will no longer perform, quite as well as it
> used to, its two principal functions: the conveyance of
> humane order which we call law, and the communica-
> tion of the quick of the human spirit which we call
> grace.[3]

3. George Steiner, *Language and Silence: Essays on Language, Literature, and the Inhuman* (New York: Atheneum, 1958, 1982), pp. 100-101.

Steiner makes two other points worth mentioning about
the consequences of language abuse: as usable words are
lost, experience becomes cruder and less communicable.
And with the loss of the subtlety, clarity, and reliability of
language, we become more vulnerable to crude exercises
of power.

Remote as we may think we are from the horrors of the
German propaganda machine, the applicability of Steiner's
concern to the condition of contemporary American English may be obvious upon brief reflection. The generation
of students coming through high schools and universities
now expect to be lied to. They know about "spin" and about
the profiteering agendas of corporate advertising. They
have grown used to the flippant, incessantly ironic banter
that passes for conversation and avoid positive claims by
verbal backpedaling: "like" before every clause that might
threaten to make a distinction one might argue with, and
"whatever" after approximations that never reach solid de-
clarative ground. They also recognize, because these corruptions have been so pervasive in their short lifetimes,
how much political discourse consists of *ad hominem* argument, accusation, smear campaigns, hyperbole, broken
promises, distortions, and lies. If they're reading many of
the mainstream news magazines and papers or watching
network television, they are receiving a daily diet of euphemisms, overgeneralizations, and evasions that pass for political and cultural analysis. Though they are being taught
in classrooms to be critical of empty rhetoric and unsup-

ported claims, the debased currency of public discourse is what is available to them, and so their own language resources are diminished and uncertain. They need our help.

I don't know how many times over the past year I've heard students, trying to make sense of the news, lament, "I don't know how to tell what to believe!" "How do I tell what's reliable?" "How do I distinguish what's true?" Their questions remind me of Wendell Berry's observation that the two epidemic illnesses of our time, "the disintegration of communities and the disintegration of persons," are closely related to the disintegration of language. "My impression," Berry writes, "is that we have seen, for perhaps a hundred and fifty years, a gradual increase in language that is either meaningless or destructive of meaning."[4]

We need to mean what we say. And for that purpose, we need to reclaim words that have been colonized and held hostage by commercial and political agencies that have riddled them with distorted meanings.

If we dig a little, we will find ourselves abundantly equipped for the task. Simply in terms of the number of available words (nearly a million), English is one of the richest languages in the world. To point this out is not to suggest that there is less value in other languages. We

4. Wendell Berry, "Standing by Words," in *Standing by Words* (Washington, D.C.: Shoemaker & Hoard, 2005), p. 14.

need them; each of them does something English can't. But more on that issue later. My primary intention here is to address readers who speak and read English most of the time, so I will focus primarily on the responsibilities of speakers of English, though the general challenge to stewardship of language applies to any speaker on earth.

Today the English language has over a million words. The average educated person knows about 20,000 words and uses about 2,000 in a week. More than half of the world's technical and scientific periodicals and three-quarters of the world's mail are in English. About 80 percent of the information stored in the world's computers is in English. English is transmitted to more than 100 million people a day by the five largest broadcasting companies.

But consider these facts about Americans who speak English:

- At least 50 percent of the unemployed are functionally illiterate (U.S. Department of Labor Statistics).
- The average kindergarten student has seen more than 5,000 hours of television, having spent more time in front of the TV than it takes to earn a bachelor's degree (Laubach Literacy Action Council). So the models of conversation they have heard have been heavily scripted in ways that allow neither in-the-moment response nor revision. Linguist Barry Sanders, among

many others, has demonstrated a direct causal relationship between early television viewing and impaired literacy.[5]

- Twenty-seven percent of army enlistees can't read training manuals written at the seventh-grade level (American Council of Life Insurance).
- One study of 21 to 25 year olds showed that 80 percent couldn't read a bus schedule, 73 percent couldn't understand a newspaper story, 63 percent couldn't follow written map directions, and 23 percent couldn't locate the gross pay-to-date amount on a paycheck stub (Laubach Literacy Action Council).
- Forty-four percent of all American adults do not read a single book in the course of a year (Literacy Volunteers of America).

Evidence for Orwell's claim that "the decline of a language must ultimately have political and economic causes" (not to mention political and economic consequences) appears to be abundant.[6] Avoiding that decline requires focused and sustained attention.

To maintain usable and reliable language — to be good stewards of words — we have at least to do these three things: (1) to deepen and sharpen our reading skills,

5. Barry Sanders, *A Is for Ox* (New York: Pantheon Books, 1994), pp. 39ff.
6. Orwell, "Politics and the English Language," p. 156.

(2) to cultivate habits of speaking and listening that foster precision and clarity, and (3) to practice *poesis* — to be makers and doers of the word. For these purposes we need regularly to exercise the tongue and the ear: to indulge in word play, to delight in metaphor, to practice specificity and accuracy, to listen critically and refuse clichés and sound bites that substitute for authentic analysis. Such deliberate focus on language is not an elitist enterprise. With over 26 million functionally illiterate people in this country, those of us who voluntarily and regularly pick up books, newspapers, and Bibles do, in fact, belong to a privileged group. Our job is not to eschew that privilege, but to use it for the sake of the whole.

The following chapters focus on "strategies of stewardship" — practices that may help to retrieve, revive, and renew our precious language resources. Here, though, if we may postpone the pleasure of positive thinking for just a few pages, I want to name more specifically the most pervasive problems we currently face in public discourse and mass media. As Thomas Hardy says, "If way to the Better there be, it exacts a full look at the Worst."[7] Think about the kinds of language abuse to which we have become accustomed — perhaps so accustomed that we cease to be offended by them: thoughtless hyperbole, un-

---

7. Thomas Hardy, "In Tenebris," in *Thomas Hardy: The Complete Poems,* ed. James Gibson (London: Macmillan & Co., 2002), p. 168.

examined metaphors, slogans and sound bites, grammatical confusion, ungrounded abstractions, overstatement, and blather. Consider, for example, how often a new product or enterprise is touted as the "best ever," a program as "really exciting," or a child's merest effort as "terrific." Or how words like *wonderful, great, fantastic, incredible,* and — most regrettably — *awesome* have progressively lost not only their original meanings but also their precision due to habitual verbal promiscuity. Consider, too, widely marketed expressions that confuse important issues — for instance, the much-bandied threat when the invasion of Iraq began to "smoke" the enemy "out of their holes," or the appropriation of "family" to describe a corporation's workforce. Or the description of war as a "job" we have to finish.

Public rhetoric is full of these dubious but consequential metaphors, and of anesthetizing phrases that postpone urgent scrutiny of national policies and public issues: "land of the free," "American way of life," "united we stand." The more candid among those who work for network news media will acknowledge that they are driven not only by corporate interests but also an audience conditioned to a shrinking attention span: many newspapers write to a fourth-grade reading level and so train readers to expect nothing more challenging. This editorial policy entails radical abbreviation of what needs careful qualification and creates a public who take their cues from — and sometimes stop at — headlines. It might give us

slight pause to remember that nineteenth-century newspapers didn't have headlines — only columns of print
that left the reader to sort out what was important in the
course of reading.

As words fall into disuse, the experiences they articulate become less accessible. Think of the wide middle
range of experience recalled in Jane Austen's novels, with
their rich vocabulary of nuance and fine distinction —
words like *agreeable, amiable, affable, genial,* and *kind* —
all sounding different affective tonalities. With the loss of
such subtleties, and of careful grammatical distinctions
(slippage in subject-verb agreement, misplaced apostro-
phes, inconsistency of tenses — mistakes that under-
mine clarity), we become more confined to the kinds of
broad strokes that make us careless and so make us care
less. Text-messaging has rapidly eroded concern for
spelling and punctuation and trains millions of users to
be content to trade precision for speed. Movements and
policies and points of view that deserve explanation are
too often summarily accepted or dismissed by a kind of
automatic sort-and-sift response to code labels and
words that end with an "ism."

With all this slippage comes a diminished range of allusion, a loss disturbingly documented in E. D. Hirsch's
controversial book *Cultural Literacy.*[8] I have found, for in-

8. E. D. Hirsch, *Cultural Literacy: What Every American Needs to
Know* (New York: Vintage Books, 1988).

stance, that in many undergraduate classes I have to explain the origins of terms like "Luddite" and "Pyrrhic victory" and "sacrificial lamb." Few Americans now take enough Latin or Greek, or even modern foreign languages, to have as much as a vestigial awareness of the etymological layers of meaning that enrich the words they use. Few of my students would recognize the kinship between "fabulous" as a descriptor for a rock concert and "fable," a tale invented to instruct and school the moral imagination.

If we recognize these trends, we must acknowledge the danger of living in what journalist Paul Weaver called "a culture of lies" where, as Steiner puts it, "Argument turns into banter, analysis into fatuous assertion."[9] The drivel that fills the airwaves — talk radio, talk shows, talk that passes for news analysis — suggests that too many of us have become willing to accept pretty much anything to stay the threat of silence: more and more talk about less and less.

Some of these abuses we not only tolerate but normalize to the point where highly questionable usages become normative. We use war language, for instance, to describe healing. We "battle" depression. We "bombard" infections with antibiotics. We want oncologists who take "aggressive measures." We use it to describe sports and, more

9. Steiner, *Language and Silence,* p. 141.

consequentially, use the language of sports, in turn, to describe war. We use it to describe work. We use it to describe our efforts to solve social problems, appropriating it even for enterprises inimical to war-making.

We inflict corrosive kinds of irony even upon the very young. From *Sesame Street* onward, sarcasm, mild insults, and ironic banter take the place of story or sustained conversation.

We allow many of the brightest among us to isolate and insulate themselves behind walls of technical, professional, and academic jargon. Higher education and academic degrees don't necessarily equip leaders to sustain functional democracy by speaking to the people with clarity, precision, and accuracy. Rather, they often become preoccupied with conversations conducted within and for the benefit of an exclusive guild. Lamenting the ways such jargon divides the experts into camps and destroys communication with the wider community, John McWhorter comments, "As long as their colleagues understand them, it wouldn't occur to the postmodernist scholar that there could be anything inappropriate in academic prose so demanding that no one can learn from it beyond their coterie, and so utterly unconcerned with euphony, rhythm, or style."[10] If this is even half-true, it is

10. John McWhorter, *Doing Our Own Thing: The Degradation of Language and Music and Why We Should, Like, Care* (New York: Gotham, 2004), p. 244.

cause for concern. We need the instruction and precise understanding that scholars and experts can provide. We need, as a public hoping to be an informed citizenry, to hold them accountable by demanding from our publicly funded institutions information and instruction that is both precise and accessible. The best of our astrophysicists, neuroscientists, and social theorists can rise to this challenge. "Accessible" is not the same as "dumbed-down."

We have appropriated the language of investment and profit to describe endeavors that ought rightly to remain distinct and free from market considerations. Self-interest and increase pervade not only "motivational" seminars in the workplace but even churches' evangelical campaigns. To a certain extent, the predisposition in favor of acquisition is built into the discourse of capitalism, and that itself deserves vigilance as long as people of faith live under the banner of enlightened self-interest. But the marketing language that dominates descriptions of human interaction in a capitalist economy obscures a much deeper understanding of the gift character of all that is, and our familial relationship to all life and especially to each other. We lose at great cost common expressions that remind us that some things cannot be bought and sold. Some times, places, relationships, and words should not be subjected to the terms of economic transaction. At least the discourse of the church should reflect this.

Normalizing the language of the marketplace within the academy and the church confuses and ultimately subverts our deepest purposes: in the one case, to promote critical thought and exchange of ideas free from coercion by those in positions of political or economic power, and in the other, to call people to something so radically different from the terms and paradigms of this world that it can be spoken of only in the variegated, complex, much-translated, much-pondered, prayerfully interpreted language of texts that have kept generations of people of faith kneeling at the threshold of unspeakable mystery and love beyond telling.

So, what are the alternatives? Market language is the dominant idiom of the culture. By way of an answer, let me return to the ecological analogy. Like food, language has been "industrialized." Words come to us processed like cheese, depleted of nutrients, flattened and packaged, artificially colored and mass marketed. And just as it takes a little extra effort and intention to find, buy, eat, and support the production of organic foods, it is a strenuous business to insist on usable, flexible, precise, enlivening language.

That is to say, in the same way that we have commodified and privatized the earth's resources — land, water, air (and, more pertinently, airwaves) — we have come to accept words as a commercial product. Just as we have become accustomed to the strip mining done on hillsides just slightly away from public thoroughfares, so we have become accustomed to practices of light camouflage that allow us to forget how the rich soil of lively discourse is being depleted.

The ecological crisis that we are facing might briefly be described in terms of three general problems. First, the ways we provide food, clothing, and shelter for ourselves in the industrialized West — methods of agricultural production, water management, fuel extraction, and resource use — have become unsustainable. Second, terms like "productivity" and "healthy economy" have obscured the idea of stewardship in ways that dull the conscience and blind the eye to practices that are fundamentally destructive of the common good. Third, the radical imbalance in resource distribution and ownership worldwide is unprecedented. "Multinational" corporations largely under North American management control a wildly disproportionate amount of the world's resources and labor. Those of us in the North American church are, as Ron Sider so eloquently put it, "rich Christians in an age of hunger."[11] Practices that benefit us directly harm and deprive others.

So, consider the analogies. Our language practices in this culture are unsustainable. We are depleting a precious resource that can only partially and slowly be re-

11. See Ron Sider, *Rich Christians in an Age of Hunger* (Nashville: W Publishing Group, 1997).

newed by active resistance to the forces at work to erode it.

The sheer volume of use is another language issue comparable to increased use of electricity, land, and fossil fuels. I have surveyed students regularly over the past several years, asking them how much silence they experience in the course of a day. Upwards of 90 percent now claim they do all their studying to background music or in the presence of background conversation. Many of them multitask as they study, fielding instant text messages and cell-phone calls while working on papers that too often exhibit the superficial thought and repetitive, imprecise language that is the inevitable result of work done under such conditions. In other words, their environment is glutted with words, sung, spoken, written, to be consumed thoughtlessly like disposable products, often becoming buffers against the pain of thought or the spiritual strenuousness of silence.

I don't say this to vilify the young or to blame them. Many of them are thoughtfully seeking a way through the morass. But they have been a "target market" their whole lives — literally, victims of corporate forces so large, relentless, and skillfully camouflaged that many of them have no sense that they are being used and abused by those who define and market privilege.

Just as they have never known a world without abundant electrical energy and electronic conveniences, so they have enjoyed less silence in their media-saturated world than any previous generation. When I teach Jane Austen, I pause over a description of the Bennett sisters' hearing the sound of horses' hooves a mile away and ask students to try to imagine the ambient silences of the early nineteenth century, where sounds were discrete and distinct, and the sounds of the natural world were not obscured by white noise. The point is this: because they hear so many words so constantly, their capacities to savor words — to pause over them, ponder them, reflect upon them, hear the echoes of ancient cadences, and attune themselves to allusiveness and alliteration — are eroding. I witness this every year.

The second part of the ecological analogy has to do with the dulling of conscience and the moral implications of careless stewardship of language. We pay a great price for our tolerance of inaccuracy and triteness.

Because of the immense influence that English wields around the globe, those of us who speak English have tremendous power and consequently tremendous responsibility. The legacy of the English Bible alone is at least equivalent to owning all the oil in the Middle East (perhaps an odious comparison). It gives its readers unequaled access to and control over the shaping of public discourse.

Consider, therefore, the implications of these facts for speakers of other tongues — for speakers of languages that have only recently emerged from predominantly oral to written cultures, for speakers of "dying" languages, and for speakers of languages and dialects restricted to local use. The very scope of English makes it a ready instrument of empire. It bears within it the imperial history of Britain and America, which includes a highly developed discourse of justification for colonialism and domination (consider terms like "errand in the wilderness," "new world," "virgin land," "manifest destiny," "advancement," and "progress") that can't be eradicated simply by legislation or policy, but need to be addressed at the level of language itself — the stories we tell ourselves about ourselves, the euphemisms in which we cloak our greed, the biases that favor the point of view of the privileged.

This brings me to my final point: Those of us who preach and teach and minister to each other need to focus on the word — on words — more explicitly, intentionally, and caringly as part of the practice of our trade. This is necessary and urgent activism: to resist "newspeak," to insist on precision and clarity, to love the bald statement, the long sentence, the particular example, the extended definition, the specifics of story, and the legacy of language we carry in our pocket Bibles and on the shelf with Shakespeare. We are stewards of the treasures that have been put into our keeping. We're not doing too well with fossil fuels and wetlands. I commend those causes to you as well. But along with them, conversation itself — the long conversation that is the warp and woof of civil and communal life — is in need of preservation and renovation.

Why Worry about Words?

Peter's admonition to "be sober, be watchful" applies to this enterprise. Noticing how things are put, noticing what is being left out or subverted, takes an active habit of mind. But what is our task as a logocentric people if not to cherish the word? God, who became, as Eliot so beautifully put it, the "word within a word, unable to speak a word," has put a measure of God's own power into our hands and on our tongues. May we use it to good purpose.

Love Words

M y favorite scene in the 1987 movie *Broadcast News* is the moment when young Aaron, who has just graduated as valedictorian of his high school class, is attacked in the schoolyard after the ceremonies by two roughnecks whose object seems to be to take him down a peg. As they run off, Aaron picks himself up and, considering how to deliver the unkindest cut possible, hollers after them by way of revenge, "You'll never know the joy of writing a graceful sentence!"

Proper care of language begins in that experience of joy. Or simply in loving the graceful sentence — loving lines like Hopkins's "He fathers forth whose beauty is past change" for their theological vision, or Frost's "For I have had too much/Of apple-picking: I am overtired/Of the great harvest I myself desired" for its quiet truth about the relinquishment that comes with age.[1] Loving the Jacobean

---

1. Gerard Manley Hopkins, "Pied Beauty," in *Poems and Prose of Gerard Manley Hopkins,* ed. W. H. Gardner (Baltimore: Penguin

language of "he maketh me to lie down in green pastures" enough not to forsake the King James Bible altogether; or Mary Oliver's insistence that "each pond with its blazing lilies/is a prayer heard and answered lavishly . . ."[2]

We gather these gifts of language as we go along — lines from poems, verses from Scripture, quips, turns of phrase, or simply words that delight us. We use them in moments of need. We share them with friends, and we reach for them in our own dark nights. They bring us into loving relationship with the large, loose "communion of saints" who have written and spoken truths that go to the heart and the gut and linger in memory. So our task as stewards of the word begins and ends in love. Loving language means cherishing it for its beauty, precision, power to enhance understanding, power to name, power to heal. And it means using words as instruments of love.

This attitude toward language does not necessarily come with education. John McWhorter, whom I cited earlier, comments on the curious loss among literate Americans of affective relationship to words — sensitivity to the aesthetic dimension of words themselves that would once have prompted compliments on a speaker's "beautiful English." "The French waiter who processes the smallest mistake as an injury to a precious artifact,"

Books, 1961), p. 30; and Robert Frost, "After Apple-Picking," in *The Poetry of Robert Frost* (New York: Holt, Rinehart & Winston, 1969), p. 68.

2. Mary Oliver, "Morning Poem," in *New and Selected Poems* (Boston: Beacon Press, 1992), p. 107.

McWhorter writes, "has a conception of his language fascinatingly distinct from ours."[3] That conception is informed by the sense that the language is a national treasure, that its subtleties and nuances, its imbedded history and the sounds that bind its dialects to land and region are to be celebrated and protected and performed, like the music of Chopin or Debussy or Poulenc.

While every language offers unique avenues of understanding and is, linguists argue, adequate to its speakers' needs, speakers of English can still, without undue pride, be grateful for the fact that we have at our disposal a repository of words and grammatical possibilities enriched by the confluence of multiple language traditions — Latin, Teutonic, Anglo-Saxon, Celtic, French, and, more recently, the languages of colonized nations throughout the British Empire. With due recognition that English bears within it the marks of an imperial past and therefore a heavy debt to peoples whose language and other resources it has appropriated and controlled, still we need to recognize the fact that this multiplicity of influences has given English "unparalleled subtlety and precision,"[4] flexibility, and texture.

In America, however, gratitude for and pride in the language of Shakespeare and Tyndale compete with a cu-

3. John McWhorter, *Doing Our Own Thing: The Degradation of Language and Music and Why We Should, Like, Care* (New York: Gotham, 2004), pp. 248-49.

4. McWhorter, *Doing Our Own Thing*, p. 164.

rious anti-intellectualism, one manifestation of a false egalitarianism that mocks the objective of true equality. The dumbing-down, oversimplification, or flattened character of public speech may make our declamations and documents more accessible, but it deprives us all of a measure of beauty and clarity that could enrich our lives together. In more and more venues where speech and writing are required, adequate is adequate. A most exhilarating denunciation of this sort of mediocrity may be found in Mark Twain's acerbic little essay, "Fenimore Cooper's Literary Offenses," in which he observes,

> When a person has a poor ear for music, he will flat and sharp right along without knowing it. He keeps near the tune, but it is *not* the tune. When a person has a poor ear for words, the result is a literary flatting and sharping; you perceive what he is intending to say, but you also perceive that he doesn't *say* it. This is Cooper. He was not a word-musician. His ear was satisfied with the *approximate* word.[5]

Yet to choose to go beyond adequate is sometimes to risk the look of elitism, the accusation of pretentiousness or pedantry.

5. Mark Twain, "Fenimore Cooper's Literary Offenses," in *The Unabridged Mark Twain*, ed. Lawrence Teacher (Philadelphia: Running Press, 1976), p. 1249.

Let us consider what "beyond adequate" looks like — what caring, careful, grateful, playful, joyful, loving use of words might entail and yield.

Several years ago I edited a little collection of essays called *Word Tastings*. The invitation to each writer who contributed an essay was to focus on a single word that he or she for any reason found intriguing, complex, haunting, curious, interestingly ambiguous, troubling, or delightful.

The essays were not academic, though some reflected on word history, usage, and lexical variations. Most of them served as reminders that the Oxford English Dictionary, used with the proper light touch, can be a source of entertainment, amusement, and surprise. These essays offered a surprising range of reflections on the richness and depth of ordinary words. I wanted to do a collection like this because it has been my experience that it is hard to get people to look *at* words instead of *through* them. When the collection came out, I began to hear from readers who, along with gratifying enthusiasm, wanted to share their own favorite words for future consideration. Everyone I heard from seemed to have a favorite word or two that merited discussion, opened floodgates of memory, or simply "tasted" good. "I don't know why — I've always just liked that word," people said about words as varied as *sycophant, asteroid, obstreperous,* and *fleece.*

These responses confirmed for me that there is, in all

of us, a hunger for words that satisfy — not just words that do the job of conveying requests or instructions or information, but words that give a pleasure akin to the pleasures of music. Most of us, most of the time, use language the way we use windows; we look "through" words to ideas, objects, sensations, landscapes of meaning. Occasionally that window glass becomes a mirror, and hearing our own words, we suddenly recognize something about ourselves. And sometimes words become objects of interest in themselves. Suddenly we notice them. We see and hear them the way poets do, as having vitality and delightfulness independent of their utility. Language may suddenly appear not as a closed system where meaning is simply constructed or a drably utilitarian system of reference, but as a dance — words at play — words not just meaning or reporting or chronicling or marching in syntactic formation, but performing themselves, sounding, echoing, evoking ripples of association and feeling, moving in curious sidelong figures rather than left to right in orderly lines. Freed of their quotidian functionality, words flit and land in odd places, or hover in the general vicinity of some thought that provides at best only a temporary resting place.

Thus at large, words, like smells, trigger memories. We all have a private vocabulary of words associated with particular moments of discovery. Psychoanalysts have built an empire on this truth simply by paying systematic attention to word associations and considering the immanent logic of the connections people make between one word and another. The fact that the word *lilac* recalls the wallpaper in a grandmother's bathroom for one, a line from Whitman for another, or a feeling of inexplicable sadness for yet another testifies to the way words constellate complex, shifting, layered patterns of meaning and feeling.

Psychoanalysts aren't the only ones who rely on this property of words for their stock in trade. Poets not only invite us but compel us to hear old words new, lure us to lower our defenses against the very associations they threaten to evoke. We expend, it seems, a good deal of mental energy daily keeping our filtering systems running, screening out the overtones, contaminants, stray strands of memory words carry. Pressed into conventional service day after day, words, like people, can degenerate and diminish; they become weary; some drop out of service altogether. Only a poetic act can restore their natural versatility, virtuosity, and capacity to surprise.

The pleasure of a word is quite distinct from the pleasure of an idea. An assignment to write about the word *piano* is likely to take us down a very different path from an article on "the piano" (the history thereof, acoustics and soundboards, pianos I have known, and so on). As any card-carrying deconstructionist will tell you, words never quite "fit" the concepts or experiences they represent. As Eliot lamented, they "slip, slide, perish,/Decay with imprecision, will not stay in place,/Will not stay still."[6] Even words for solid, sensible objects — *ball, saxophone, lake* — become trailheads for surprising and circuitous journeys through memory, association, and the back roads of lexicography. But if those journeys leave readers "tasting" their own words, loving them for their pungency, their sharpness, their smoothness, or even their sting, then the dictionaries have served their purposes and something worthwhile has been preserved.

The pleasure of savoring words cannot be attained without some reclamation work. Words have to be "taken back," brushed off, and sometimes healed. The business of reclaiming words from gradual erosion might be seen as a project in species preservation. English — American English in particular, as we have said — has already suffered severe losses in a spreading epidemic of hyperbole. Streamlined and simplified newspapers and textbooks have forced fewer and fewer words to serve the purposes of public discourse, so we sustain losses in nuance and precision whose consequences have not yet been fully recognized.

When a word falls into disuse, the experience goes with it. We are impoverished not only by the loss of a precise descriptor, but by the atrophy and extinction of the

6. T. S. Eliot, *Burnt Norton,* in *The Complete Poems and Plays of T. S. Eliot* (New York: Harcourt, Brace & World, 1971), p. 121.

very thing it describes. Think about grand old words like *proper, prudent, sensible, noble, honorable,* and *merry.* Have you ever heard a friend returning from a party describe how merry it was? Unless you're very, very old, I suspect not. The word survives in American usage almost exclusively as a vestigial reminder of certain obligatory feelings of good cheer around Christmastime. But merriment itself seems to belong to a place beyond the looking glass — something we can imagine wistfully as we step into the world of Austen or Dickens, but can't bring back into the milieu of the contemporary cocktail party. Merriment seems to evoke two conditions of community life we have largely lost: a common sense of what there is to laugh about, and a certain mental health — what William James would have called "healthy-mindedness" — that understands darkness, but doesn't succumb to cynicism. Merriment has fallen into near extinction by a disuse that both signals and hastens the demise of such attitudes. Wendell Berry's writing offers examples of such language reclaimed and put to good use for contemporary purposes. Without pretension he retrieves words like *provident, kinsmen, courtship, mirth,* and *chastisement.*

Let us pause here and reflect on one example of this kind of casualty. *Felicity* is a good case in point — a loss to the language of emotional life whose disappearance deprives us of a particular dimension of happiness. Felicity is a kind of happiness our culture does not, on the whole, promote: something like rational contentment, entailing acceptance, considered compromise, and self-knowledge. When Elizabeth Bennett, Jane Austen's intelligent and critical-minded heroine, listens to her sister's suitor pouring out his hopes for his own and his beloved's happiness, the author writes of her,

> ... she had to listen to all he had to say, of his own happiness, and of Jane's perfections; and in spite of his being a lover, Elizabeth really believed all his expectations of felicity to be rationally founded, because they had for basis the excellent understanding, and superexcellent disposition, of Jane, and a general similarity of feeling and taste between her and himself.[7]

This kind of considered happiness, pursued with a clear eye toward economic stability, compatible temperament, and self-control, contrasts sharply with the kind of happiness marketed in movies that focus on falling in love against all odds, throwing caution to the winds, following the passions, and losing oneself in a rush of sensation. Felicity has more to do with finding oneself.

The word has a venerable history. From the Latin *felix*, it is linked in the liturgy of the Latin mass with the good that comes out of and in spite of evil: "*O Felix culpa . . .*" — "O blessed fault, O happy sin of Adam, that

---

7. Jane Austen, *Pride and Prejudice* (1813; New York: Random House, Bantam Dell edition, 2003), p. 357.

merited such a redeemer. . . ." In this instance, happiness is an unexpected gift, only recognized as happiness in long retrospect, paradoxical in the way it is linked to pain and loss. Like the old rabbi in a traditional Hasidic tale who responded to tales of triumph with "How do you know it's not a disaster?" and to tales of misfortune with "How do you know it's not a blessing?" the person who understands felicity understands that happiness changes as it ripens, and that the unripe fruit is often bitter.

Happiness of this kind is, in fact, more a point of view than a state of affairs. When I told a dejected young student recently that I thought happiness was often a matter of deciding to be happy, she looked at me as if I was not only cold-hearted and unsympathetic, but couldn't possibly, with such an attitude, have a clue about what disappointment felt like. Such observations can sound glib, I admit. Yet I think they can be much-needed correctives to the commodified notion of happiness that links it so insistently with getting, spending, having, consuming, and receiving the blessings of privilege without much reference to the burdens of payment. There's not much glamour in contentment, or much dramatic value, which may be the payoff that keeps some people in a state of perpetual crisis and discontent. But contentment is more durable than excitement or the quick thrill and, like rich soil that has been given necessary fallow time, may equip a person for a fuller harvest of satisfactions and a longer period of productivity than the synthetic quick fix of instant satisfaction.

But felicity includes something beyond simple contentment. Felicity not only accepts what is, acknowledging and cheerfully submitting to the limitations of one's condition; it also unabashedly wills and seeks pleasure. Its pleasures are more subtle than sensational. Felicity comes in lively, sustained conversation; in long walks on which one notices small changes in the landscape; in the silent companionship of an old friend or partner; in serving a good dinner to a family one loves. Felicity seeks happiness actively, but its actions are quiet and measured rather than flamboyant and impulsive. It deepens by having reflected enough on one's own good to realize that one's own good consists in appreciation and service of others.

I think of felicity as a sign of wisdom. The handful of people I know who I would call truly wise are also happy, and the particular quality of happiness they have in common is felicity. They love a good story that makes a point as it makes you laugh. They live simply, but not meanly, and love to lift the lid of the soup pot and savor the smell of vegetables mingling. They love good company and cherish solitude. They care for children unsentimentally and do not spoil them. They are able to say no to what does not suit their purposes. They are, in their various ways, markedly articulate.

This last item may seem unlike the rest: Why would happiness have anything to do with being articulate? Yet when we talk about "felicity of expression" (a common usage cited in the Random House Dictionary), we link happiness to skill — specifically to verbal skill. A felicitous word choice is one that so precisely names an idea or experience that it produces for the reader or hearer a shock of recognition, a surprised "Yes! That's it!" and a gratifying sense of having put two interlocking pieces of a puzzling world perfectly in place.

Precision of expression is neither taught nor appreciated in a culture that has prostituted language in the service of propaganda. To the degree that we consent to cheap hyperbole, flip slogans, and comfortably unexamined claims, we deprive ourselves of the felicity of expression that brings things worth looking at into focus — things like happiness, for instance, which comes so much clearer and seems so much richer when we see it displayed in an array of colors: merriment, blitheness, gaiety, delight, contentment, joy, bliss, felicity itself. But perhaps, if what I told my student is true, that happiness is a decision. We can fall prey to the flattening of words and experience, and so diminish the variety and quality of happiness, or we can retrieve the words that name the forms of happiness that are worth pursuing and, by returning them to good and careful use, rediscover felicity.

Felicity of expression, however, requires a certain amount of unglamorous detail work. One of the minor annoyances associated with being introduced as an English teacher is the frequent, by-now unfunny response,

"Oh — well, then, I'd better watch my grammar." I'm tempted these days, rather than deflecting such inanities with weak, polite laughter, to take on the schoolmarmy stereotype and answer, "Yes, you'd better!" I am moved, while speaking of love of language, to say a kind word for subordinate clauses and semicolons and for versatile participles and verbs that give honest accountings of process.

A dear colleague to whom I take my occasional uncertainties about etymology and grammatical conundrums commented, after musing over an oddly unclassifiable construction, "Every grammar leaks." The rules of grammar as we know them don't account for all linguistic possibilities; they offer a map of relations in something like the way Newton's physics accounts for a fair range of phenomena, but falls short of Einstein's more adequate paradigm. Indeed, as Barry Sanders points out, "Breaking the hold that simple grammatical construction has on language [as in poetry] permits us to gain a fresh insight on old things — everyday experience, commonplace ideas — in a radically new way."[8] Moreover, linguists not only have changed the terms in which we were taught to describe the relations of words to one another, but widely dispute the notion of "correct" grammar as a concept that overlooks the inherent fluidity, liveliness,

8. Barry Sanders, *A Is for Ox* (New York: Pantheon Books, 1994), p. 66.

and invention of spoken language. "Ebonics," or black English, with its curiously Jacobean constructions and vestiges of authentic oral culture, is a case in point, and one not to be dismissed. Street speech in our urban cultures, like the local dialects of peasant cultures, makes its own contribution to revitalizing the music of language and refocusing our hearing.

But simple ignorance of basic grammatical understanding is not in itself a virtue. And I still believe that respect for the ability to apply well the rhetorical power of skillfully constructed sentences is, in fact, a mark of both intelligence and grace. This is not the place or time for a theory of grammar, but I do want to pause and celebrate, individually, the invaluable work that is accomplished in their decent and orderly way by particular parts of speech.

First, the preposition, which we love for its startling power to affirm and reframe relationships. Think, for instance, how much prepositional theology is imbedded in the words of the hymn taken from an ancient Celtic prayer, "St. Patrick's Breastplate":

> Christ be with me, Christ within me,
> Christ behind me, Christ before me,
> Christ beside me, Christ to win me,
> Christ to comfort and restore me.
> Christ beneath me, Christ above me,
> Christ in quiet, Christ in danger,

Love Words

Christ in hearts of all that love me,
Christ in mouth of friend and stranger.

Each of those prepositions — *with, within, behind, before,
beside, beneath, above,* and *in* — opens an avenue of reflection on the mysterious and manifold nature of relationship to Christ — how Christ leads, accompanies,
backs us up, holds us up, protects, sustains, indwells. Or
think of the rhetorical formula we cling to as Americans
who still share some common vision of constitutional democracy in "a government of the people, by the people,
and for the people," each preposition its own chapter in
political theory, bearing its own vision of justice. It may
be that we have our regional differences about whether
we stand "in" line or "on" line, and there may be some play
of meaning around what's "in" and what's definitely "not
on," but even at their most idiosyncratic, prepositions do
good service in the ways they locate and organize and
help us, as Henry James put it, to "understand things in
relation," which, he claimed, is the only way they can be
rightly understood.

And let's hear a little praise for the undersung con-
junctions that hold together the parts of things until we
can envision the whole. Those that subordinate give us
whole theories of history: *because* and *since* and *although*
excusing or indicting in swift, single strokes the decisions
of kings or the deceptions of demagogues, explaining the
fall of Rome or the czar's victory over a foolish emperor.

And even the lowly coordinators *and, but,* and *or* pry away the blinders that would let us see anything in isolation.

And the modifiers — overused, hackneyed, and redundant as they often are — can sharpen our vision like lenses. Spacious and squalid, darkling and sullen, luminous and undulant, they give us tools to distinguish and compare and somehow grasp the qualities that might otherwise escape the eye or the searching heart.

And nouns — those instruments of Adam's power. All those Peterson's Guides that give us the names of flora and fauna, the apples and balls and cats that launched us on our alphabetical way, the visual dictionaries that assure us that every screw and bolt and thingamajig has a legitimate name, reaffirm the solidity and stability and security we find in the names of persons, places, and things. Deconstruction notwithstanding, we do rely on the relations between words and things. As Wendell Berry puts it in *Standing by Words,* the "relation of speaker, word, and object must be conventional; the community must know what it is."[9] We even affirm the goodness of young parents' freedom to name their children after trees or honeymoon resorts or rock stars because they have taken part in the work of creation, and the gift of naming is a commensurate reward. Mere lists

9. Wendell Berry, "Standing by Words," in *Standing by Words* (Washington, D.C.: Shoemaker & Hoard, 2005), p. 25.

of nouns can be poetry. Think, for example, of Hopkins's exuberant inventory in "Pied Beauty":

> Glory be to God for dappled things —
>> For skies of couple-colour as a brinded cow;
>>> For rose-moles all in stipple upon trout that swim;
> Fresh-firecoal chestnut-falls; finches' wings;
>> Landscape plotted & pieced — fold, fallow, & plough;
>>> And all trades, their gear & tackle & trim.[10]

He ends, of course, with a cry of praise for the one who fittingly "fathers forth" all this abundance of particulars.

So we love nouns and the material blessings they bestow. But most of all I want before we leave this little tour of parts of speech to give thanks for verbs. We depend on them to reveal the dance of the whole dynamic universe, from orbiting electrons to sucking undertows to swiftly tilting planets. We entwine them in sentences like strands to describe the complex weave of events. A single verb can change our sense of what it is we are witnessing, as when Mary Oliver writes of preying vultures, "they minister to the grassy miles."[11] Good verbs invest our gestures with the language of the heart. Recall Frost: "There were ten thousand thousand fruit to touch,/cherish in

10. Hopkins, "Pied Beauty," p. 30.
11. Mary Oliver, "Vultures," in *New and Selected Poems,* p. 155.

hand, lift down, and not let fall."[12] And sometimes nouns become verbs because they can't sit still any longer: so things catapult and flame, and meetings are chaired. Verbs, I think, matter most. <u>Asked for his name, God gave Moses a verb</u>. And even those of us who are, as Cummings put it, "human merely being" can't be contained in nouns, even buttressed by the best adjectives, but burst and blossom into verbs like Van Gogh's trees and leaping fields when we are most alive.

We care for words when we use them thankfully, recognizing in each kind a specific gift borne in the mother tongue, bestowed at birth as a legacy from the one who was, in the beginning, with God, who was God.

12. Frost, "After Apple-Picking."

Tell the Truth

"Tell all the truth, but tell it slant . . ." is Emily Dickinson's advice.[1] It may be that her words are not just counsel about how to achieve the success that "in circuit lies," but an acknowledgment that we have no choice but to tell truth "slant." We see only one side of the elephant at a time. So perhaps the best we can do in our efforts to tell the truth is to take the measure of our own slant on it and be accountable for our points of view.

I've been struck by how often slant is confused with bias — as though having a point of view, a set of assumptions, or a firmly held opinion is in itself unscrupulous or unfair. And as though neutrality is the mark of fairness or truth. But opinions are the stock-in-trade of thoughtful people, to be earned and held strongly until further evidence requires their modification. Perhaps suspicion of

1. Emily Dickinson, "Tell All the Truth," in *Complete Poems of Emily Dickinson,* ed. Thomas Johnson (Boston: Little, Brown, 1960), p. 506.

opinion, or the hesitancy to form one (reflected in the all-too-frequent sentence trailer, "Whatever . . .") comes from long exposure to opinions aired too soon on too little evidence, adopted without argument, for purposes of private gain. Opinions are selling points or sticking points more often than points of departure from which one takes stock before embarking on further investigation or reflection.

Truth-telling is difficult because the varieties of untruth are so many and so well disguised. Lies are hard to identify when they come in the form of apparently innocuous imprecision, socially acceptable slippage, hyperbole masquerading as enthusiasm, or well-placed propaganda. These forms of falsehood are so common, and even so normal, in media-saturated, corporately controlled culture that truth often looks pale, understated, alarmist, rude, or indecisive by comparison. Flannery O'Connor's much-quoted line "You shall know the truth, and the truth shall make you odd" has a certain prophetic force in the face of more and more commonly accepted facsimiles of truth — from PR to advertising claims to propaganda masquerading as news.

In the face of those deceptions, the business of telling the truth, and caring for the words we need for that purpose, is more challenging than ever before. Simply the scale on which lies can be and are propagated can be overwhelming. So let us reflect here on the practice of precision as a spiritual discipline that lies at the heart of truth-telling and of the faithful stewardship of words.

First, a list. I like lists. So I made a list of characteristics that seem to me to help distinguish truth from its many facsimiles:

Truth is elusive.
Truth avoids institutional control.
Truth tugs at conventional syntax.
Truth hovers at the edge of the visual field.
Truth is relational.
Truth lives in the library and on the subway.
Truth is not two-sided; it's many-sided.
Truth burrows in the body.
Truth flickers.
Truth comes on little cat's feet, and down back alleys.
Truth doesn't always test well.
Truth invites you back for another look.

My hope is that this list will help frame and complicate our discussion of truth-telling with a sense of the challenges it entails.

It can be hard to maintain a sense of and be faithful to the complexities of any issue that matters. Serving on a committee recently to review a piece of publicity material for a local organization, I registered strenuous objections to the clichés and vapid abstractions that seemed to bury the main points (such as they were) in wet cotton. "This is what works," was the reply. "This is what PR writing looks like. It reassures people." I will not record here the umbrage I took at this bland pragmatism. I left the committee meeting darkly convinced that people who buy (and buy into) prose with no sinews, atrophied syntax, emaciated metaphors, and calculated imprecision deserve what they get.

But there is no question that precision is difficult to achieve. Imprecision is easier. Imprecision is available in a wide variety of attractive and user-friendly forms: clichés, abstractions and generalizations, jargon, passive constructions, hyperbole, sentimentality, and reassuring absolutes. Imprecision minimizes discomfort and creates a big, soft, hospitable place for all opinions; even the completely vacuous can find a welcome there. So the practice of precision not only requires attentiveness and effort; it may also require the courage to afflict the comfortable and, consequently, tolerate their resentment.

Precision begins with defining terms. Recently I asked a group of students to write down their working definitions of five terms whose imprecise usage these days poses a serious threat to peace and safety: *liberal, conservative, patriotic, terrorist,* and *Christian.* The results were sobering in their range and banality. We have all witnessed the abuses of these terms — the ways in which they are co-opted to serve particular partisan agendas and to prevent serious discussion of particulars. If patriots could be required to specify which particular U.S. policies they support and why, we might have some talking points. If the "Christian right" would acknowledge the existence of a Christian left, the community of believers might be able to deliver a lively witness to the capaciousness of our faith in spirited (and I used that term advisedly) debate.

The business of definition, of course, takes us well beyond mere lexical considerations. Precision means attending to the ways the word is used, not merely to some notion of how it should be used. It means humbly inquiring what the user means, and then listening. Paradoxically, precision also requires leaving some play in the matter of definition and negotiating precise meaning as discussion proceeds. We may have to accept "for the sake of argument" a definition of "socialism" or "acceptable deviation" or "appropriate precautions" with which we don't fully agree in order to create a context of understanding that enables truth to be spoken, heard, and acted on.

Precision also requires attention to process. If I had to name one of the most urgent goals I pursue in writing courses, it is the use of precise verbs — finding the verb that clarifies the subtleties or intricacies of process. Using the exact word and not, as Twain puts it, "its second cousin." If your verbs are precise, I tell students, if they get at who did what to whom in what way as specifically as possible, your writing will improve by 50 percent. (I made up the statistic, as I also tell them. I'm precise with words. Numbers are another matter. . . .) It is hard to think clearly about process in an environment where most of us are surrounded with products we did not participate in planting, harvesting, designing, manufacturing, transporting, or marketing. Indeed, the processes by which things come to us are often deliberately hidden or left unmentioned so as not to draw attention to the less savory aspects of process like pollution, abusive labor practices, fuel consumption, dangerous pesticides, unfair treatment of animals, insider trading. So a precise use of the term *cost* would include all of the above — would perhaps enlarge to Thoreau's definition: "I count the cost of a thing in terms of how much of life I have to give to obtain it."

Certainly one of the most consequential areas in which imprecision is both commonplace and deliberate is in the justification of violence and injustice. Any one of us, for example, could quickly come up with a lengthy list of euphemisms designed to obscure the processes and costs of war. Think of how the term "collateral damage" spares us the discomfort of imagining the bodies of women and children ripped open by the explosions of "smart bombs" that destroy everything within a 120-foot radius of their target.

Wendell Berry's short story "Making It Home" offers a memorable experiment in truth-telling about war. In it Berry undertakes to describe in plain language the experience of a soldier returning from battle:

The fighting had been like work, only a lot of people got killed and a lot of things got destroyed. It was not work that *made* much of anything. You and your people intended to go your way, if you could. And you wanted to stop the other people from going their way, if you could. And whatever interfered you destroyed. You had a thing on your mind that you wanted, or wanted to get to, and anything at all that stood in your way, you had the right to destroy. If what was in the way were women and little children, you would not even know it, and it was all the same. When your power is in a big gun, you don't have any small intentions. Whatever you want to hit, you want to make dust out of it. Farms, houses, whole towns — things that people had made well and cared for a long time — you made nothing of. . . . You got to where you could not look at a man without knowing how little it would take to kill him. For a man was nothing but just a little morsel of soft flesh and brittle bone inside of some clothes. And you could not look at a house or a schoolhouse or a church without knowing how, rightly hit, it would just shake down inside itself into a pile of stones and ashes.[2]

This representation of the altered state of awareness, the "zone" in which a soldier might insulate himself from

2. Wendell Berry, "Making It Home," in *Fidelity: Five Stories* (New York: Pantheon, 1993), pp. 86, 88.

the pain he inflicts and the guilt it might bring, relies for its impact on simple language: verbs like *kill, destroy, hit,* and *want,* and nouns like *morsel, bone, dust, stones,* and *ashes.* The precision of language has to do not with sophistication, but rather with the felt accuracy of elemental feelings and appetites. This kind of precision is both accusation and confession. It is strenuous and highly morally relevant — hardly a matter reducible to the aesthetics of style. Precision like this produces what Edmund Wilson called a "shock of recognition," or what we still invoke as a "ring of truth." It is tested against our own memories of fear and numbness and moments of crude will to power.

Notice how part of the power of precision lies in understatement. There is no report of explosions, no wide-angle vision of a devastated landscape, no cries of the dying. Berry's work is exemplary in its resistance to the temptations of hyperbole. Those temptations are particularly acute in a marketing environment where competition for the attention of an audience (or a client or a customer) puts us all in the position of Lear's daughters, competing for the kingdom. We who are speakers and writers of American English can learn a great deal about the value and power of understatement from the British. Their delightful dry humor relies on it, their press is still to some degree held in check by it, and, along with the crown jewels, they hold claim to Jane Austen, whose dual legacy of precision and restraint is a gift to us all.

48

Lest this all sound simply crusty, curmudgeonly, or jaundiced, let me take brief account of what I think we stand to lose by embracing the culture of hyperbole. We lose our countercultural edge. Biblical wisdom calls us to be countercultural — to be in the world, but not of it. To be in the world is to be socially and politically engaged, to work for the kingdom here and now, recognizing that it is within us and among us. But to be of it is to accept its terms, its currencies, its objectives and agendas as legitimate, and to allow them to delimit and sometimes determine our own. That is capitulation. And if hyperbole is not a cause, it is at least a symptom of such capitulation. It may be that the intention is to appropriate the power of "media speak" and redirect it to good ends, but the medium does become the message, and at great cost.

One of the most egregious examples of this substitution of hyperbole for clarity and precision is the recent publication of the New Testament in magazine versions — one for girls, one for "guys," designed to imitate the visual appeal of *Cosmopolitan, Seventeen,* and *Hot Rod.* (I actually grudgingly acquired used copies to circulate for critical scrutiny on appropriate occasions.) Bold colors, large-type assertions, sidebars, and photographs of young people with conventionally perfect bodies and teeth overwhelm the text that is the New Century version of the New Testament. It requires some effort for the eye to remain fixed on the text itself against the ubiquitous visual distractions that compete with it.

This brings us to another loss. In a similar if less painfully obvious way, the discourse of the church, the subtleties of biblical language and sensitivity to nuances of translation, the ear for poetry and care for theological distinctions may be eroded by allowing media language to become the dialect of our worship and fellowship.

I say this not only as a warning against what I think diminishes and damages the treasures that are ours to care for, but also as an invitation to help one another maintain the more strenuous pleasures of precision, clarity, lively confrontation, and mutual empowerment. Certainly what we see modeled in Austen's novels are all of those features of community life. We see these, by the way, in many private letters of the time, lest you be tempted to think Elizabeth's articulate arguments with Darcy are merely the stuff of effete fiction. In a culture of courtesy, one could afford confrontation. In a culture of restraint, a sharp and well-aimed word went a long way. Darcy, if you recall, is driven to soul-searching and a significant change of heart when it is pointed out that he did not behave in a "gentlemanly manner." For him, the term *gentleman* carried a heavy and binding burden of obligation, understood and accepted.

In reading a recent novel, I myself was convicted by a comment the mother makes to her adult daughter: "My dear, you've missed so many opportunities to say nothing." We do miss those opportunities, as well as opportunities to say less and say it more judiciously. And so we miss the particular delights of finding words and speaking them into silences big enough to allow them to be heard.

Finally, if we give way to hyperbole — and to the comparable temptations of sentimentality, slogans, and other kinds of language designed to "sell" — we lose credibility. Corporations with multimillion-dollar marketing budgets are better at devising and using those instruments of persuasion. I suggest we let them have them and remember the persuasiveness of the "still small voice" that speaks beneath the whirlwind.

Precision is, after all, not only a form of responsibility and a kind of pleasure, but an instrument of compassion. To be precise requires care, time, and attention to the person, place, or process being described. Consider, for instance, the quality of insight reflected in this description of a grandmother in Marilynne Robinson's exquisitely written novel *Housekeeping:*

> She was then a magisterial woman, not only because of her height and her large, sharp face, not only because of her upbringing, but also because it suited her purpose, to be what she seemed to be so that her children would never be startled or surprised, and to take on all the postures and vestments of matron, to differentiate her life from theirs, so that her children would never feel intruded upon. Her love for them was utter and equal, her government of them generous and absolute. She was constant as daylight, and she would be unre-

marked as daylight, just to watch the calm inwardness of their faces.[3]

Three "becauses" remind us that there is intention behind what we see in this "magisterial" woman. And that startling, large adjective links her to queenly presences we've been given to imagine: Bathsheba, Cleopatra, Elizabeth I, Victoria. Her purposes are understood in terms of deep and sensitive attention to the lives and needs of her children: modulation and moderation of her own considerable power for their sakes, deliberate restraint designed to give them room for uninvaded "inwardness." The whole description invites us to understand the grandmother in terms of her highly nuanced processes of reasoning and feeling and the children she raises in terms of their vulnerability and possibility. But words like *large* and *sharp* forestall any inclination to soften the force of the character described. Like the dark shading strokes that give a life drawing its character, a few words give this image an edge and a shadow and remind us that she might easily have been very different and harsher had she not given thought to her purposes and effects.

Like a true account of character, a true account of process requires a reckoning of particulars. Annie Dillard opens a chapter titled "Intricacy" with a dazzlingly rich

---

3. Marilynne Robinson, *Housekeeping* (New York: Picador, reprint edition, 2004), pp. 28-29.

description of light coming in a kitchen window. Its precise and startling verb choices reclaim from ordinariness what is and should be a daily source of amazement:

A rosy, complex light fills my kitchen at the end of these lengthening June days. From an explosion on a nearby star eight minutes ago, the light zips through space, particle-wave, strikes the planet, angles on the continent, and filters through a mesh of land dust: clay bits, sod bits, tiny wind-borne insects, bacteria, shreds of wing and leg, gravel dust, grits of carbon, and dried cells of grass, bark, and leaves. Reddened, the light inclines into this valley over the green western mountains; it sifts between pine needles on northern slopes, and through all the mountain blackjack oak and haw, whose leaves are unclenching, one by one, and making an intricate, toothed and lobed haze. The light crosses the valley, threads through the screen on my open kitchen window, and gilds the painted wall. A plank of brightness bends from the wall and extends over the goldfish bowl on the table where I sit.[4]

Like Thoreau before her, Dillard manages to sustain a simultaneous awareness of the minute and the immense, to challenge conventional categories of perception, and

4. Annie Dillard, "Intricacy," in *Pilgrim at Tinker Creek* (New York: Harper & Row, 1974; Perennial Classics edition, 1998), p. 123.

to find verbs that attune us to the staggering speed and complexity, and even the wild unlikelihood of what we have learned to reduce to visual object or unremarkable event. Light that zips and strikes and angles and inclines, becoming toothed and lobed and resolving into a plank, thrusts us into appropriate awe even as we laugh over the incongruity of the goldfish bowl receiving the force of such blessing. Paradox and ambiguity are fully acknowledged as one sentence begins not where the previous one left off, but somehow anew, trying again to get at what is so fast, unfathomable, and deceptively still. Nouns and verbs do all they can to help us imagine, and they succeed wonderfully in reminding us that finally we cannot. Not quite. Not ever. Because we live in mystery. So precision requires not only close and patient observation, but also daring imagination and what Keats called "negative capability" — the capacity to dwell in paradox or ambiguity without straining after resolution. To inhabit, as it were, two dimensions or points of view at once, and calmly.

These are some of the demands of truth-telling. Stewardship of words is a high calling, though not one that can be relegated to professionals. We are all called to be responsible hearers, speakers, and doers of the word. Still, telling the truth is something like an extreme sport for the very committed. The weather is never predictable, and there is always an undertow. We learn, gradually, from those who do it well, how to tolerate the "intolerable wrestle with words and meanings," as Eliot put it, and even to delight in it. We calibrate the differences between what we want words to mean and how they may be heard; we pick them up from the dusty corners where most of the good ones have been consigned to disuse and re-introduce them, hoping to ambush the listener who is contented with cliché. Like Adrienne Rich, who called herself "a woman sworn to lucidity," we pledge our energies to the work of smithing words for purposes they have never before had to serve. We temper our urgencies (if we are inclined to prophesy) with play because no responsible word work can happen without it, or without the act of trust it takes to leave the keyboard and gaze at palm trees leaning in the wind while waiting for a good verb.

Precision is possible, even though words do slip and slide. Precise language surprises like a dancer's extra second of stillness in mid-air; word and experience come together in an irreproducible moment of epiphanic delight. The next time the word appears, it may have a different feel or color or emphasis. Contexts change; usage changes; assigned meaning shifts; words accrue rings of history like trees and become more dense with life. This density contributes to their usefulness and beauty; they resonate with overtones from earlier times. They bring strong residues of cultural experience with them. They evoke whole poems: "linnet" can recall Yeats's "Lake Isle of Innisfree"; "tempests" can take us straight to a Shakespearean sonnet; and no mention of a "dark wood" has been the same since Dante.

Don't Tolerate Lies

Having considered our responsibilities as stewards of language to use words carefully, precisely, and truthfully, I'd like now to consider a dimension of that responsibility that may be a little more challenging: the responsibility not to tolerate lies. It has become commonplace to observe, as I have several times earlier, that we live in a culture where various forms of deception are not only commonly practiced but commonly accepted. And most of us, at least some of the time, object — at least to the lies that vilify our party or candidate or misrepresent our causes, and at least to each other over coffee or dinner — or we talk back to the talk-show host in the privacy of our cars. But I'd like to suggest that if we don't take our complaints further than that, we're part of the problem. Indeed, we bear a heavy responsibility for allowing ourselves to be lied to. As Pascal pointed out long before the age of media spin, "We hate the truth, and people hide it from us; we want to be flattered, and people flatter us; we like being de-

56

ceived, and we are deceived."[1] The deceptions we particularly seem to want are those that comfort, insulate, legitimate, and provide ready excuses for inaction.

Again, let me invoke the ecological analogy. If we purchase food and other products whose processing or manufacture involves unethical use of resources or human labor, our participation in those systems is not ethically neutral. If we boycott or protest unjust practices, we may not stop the practices, but we add to what may become a critical mass of resistance and, in however modest a way, support the change we hope for. This seems like fairly obvious reasoning. What is less obvious is the extension of this reasoning to language practices. The analogy may carry more weight if we consider specifically what we all stand to lose when lies are tolerated. Lies that make their way into policy decisions, campaigns, and marketing strategies erode the social contract that enables us all to count on what we've called professional ethics, business ethics, and the commitments that public servants make when they take oaths of office.

I'm not naïve enough to think there ever was a time when public office was free of calculated misrepresentations, broken promises, and organized deceptions. What has changed is both the scale of such offenses and the attitude of the public toward them. Tolerance may not be

---

1. Blaise Pascal, *Pensées,* trans. A. J. Krailsheimer (New York: Penguin Classics, reissue edition, 1995), p. 326.

the right term. It may simply be passivity. Or a species of fatigue in the face of the mountains of information, misinformation, disinformation, and trivia that requires sorting out if we're going to pursue the truth of even one significant narrative in the stream of current events. Televangelists turn Scripture to unscrupulous and self-interested ends. Politicians engage in insider trading, drape mantles of respectability around war profiteering, and construct legitimizing narratives to mask power-mongering. Occasionally a scandal erupts. The Bay of Pigs. The Gulf of Tonkin. Watergate. Jim and Tammy Faye Bakker. Monica Lewinsky. Enron. Illegal wiretapping. Torture. Then the noise dies down. Particularly in an environment of closely held, corporately controlled media, it is hard to amass enough solid evidence to hold public servants accountable — in Wendell Berry's phrase, to demand that they stand by their words.

So what, then? Do we shrug and say there's nothing we can do? I don't think so. It seems to me that the call to be stewards of words requires of us some willingness to call liars to account — particularly when their lies threaten the welfare of the community. Certainly we need to do this with humility, aware of the ways in which each one of us has a heart that is "deceitful above all things, and desperately wicked" (Jer. 17:9). (It's not always expedient, I suppose, to be quite as forthright as Al Franken, whose recent book *Lies and the Lying Liars Who Tell Them* draws a rather dramatic line in the sands of public debate!) Still, if there is to be health in the body politic and in the Body of Christ, healing involves naming the insults and offenses. It involves holding each other and our leaders accountable. It means clarifying where there is confusion; naming where there is evasion; correcting where there is error; fine-tuning where there is imprecision; satirizing where there is folly; changing the terms when the terms falsify.

The question is how to go about carrying out such complex responsibilities. What is true? This is not a rhetorical question to ask while we wash our hands like Pontius Pilate. This is a homework question to ask when we browse at a newsstand or channel surf, looking for reliable reporting. It is a question more than one voter has asked when considering how to vote responsibly in a very fallible if not corrupt system. How do we inform ourselves and listen for truth? As a character in Hermann Hesse's *Steppenwolf* suggests, we must listen through the noise to the music.[2] We must listen with all our might, with all our will to discern, laying aside our very human desire to be right with a prayer that we may be faithful.

Any effort to find reliable reporting needs to start not with questions about the sources but with questions about ourselves. What are my responsibilities as a citi-

2. Hermann Hesse, *Steppenwolf* (New York: Picador, reprint edition, 2002), p. 216.

zen? As a person of faith? As a consumer? As a leader? As a parent? As an educator? What am I avoiding knowing? Why? What point of view am I protecting? Why? How have I arrived at my assumptions about what sources of information to rely on? What limits my angle of vision? Have I tried to imagine how one might arrive at a different conclusion? How much evidence do I need to be convinced? What kind of persuasion works most effectively for me? How do I accredit or challenge authority?

The answers to these questions are not simply personal. Some of them involve serious theological reflection on the relationship between the Kingdom of God and the state, what it means to give Caesar what is Caesar's and God what is God's, and whether and how to participate in the conduct of worldly affairs. If you're Mennonite or Amish, that boundary is drawn pretty clearly. But most of us, I think, are navigating the murky middle ground marked out between not-so-separate church and state, trying to resist manipulation, seek truth, and act on it justly in the ways that remain open to us.

So let us restrict our consideration for a moment to the matter of reading or hearing the news. Constitutional democracy depends on an informed citizenry. In the world as we know it, even Christian separatists depend upon some public narrative to act in ways that serve peace and justice. So, as we look for that narrative thread among mountains of sensationalistic, biased, partisan, or simply incompetent or incomplete reporting, we need to equip ourselves with usable criteria of discernment.

Here, for instance, are some questions to pose about news sources before investing our trust in them:

Who are the sponsors, and what are their vested interests? What is their track record?

Who is framing the questions? What questions are conspicuously not being addressed — or being consigned to a back page, or a subordinate clause? Who is selecting? Sequencing? Explaining?

Are there detectable partisan biases in the language used to describe events or decisions? Euphemisms? Slogans? Abstractions that elide specific processes and effects? Value-laden metaphors?

What authorities are appealed to? What are their credentials and allegiances? Who is getting paid by whom in the process of publication?

How much information is sufficient to allow me to take a position? To support or resist a policy that has implications for other human beings? Whose is the burden of proof? What is my burden?

These questions take time to address — more time, probably, than any one of us has, which is why I would suggest that we help one another. We are called not only individually but collectively to care for the words we share and exchange. Now more than ever, reading groups, discussion groups, and Web sites where information can be shared and pondered among folk who trust one another's purposes may be helpful in enabling us to survive the tidal wave of contaminated information. Such groups are useful in their complementarity. Natural gullibility or cynicism may be tempered by reason. One's rigid rationalism may be nuanced by another's language of feeling and intuition.

Our goal is to be, together, wise as serpents and harmless as doves. The first requires healthy suspicion, understanding of process, historical perspective, and, more to our point, attentiveness to uses and abuses of language. The second requires mutual support in the arduous business of seeking peace as well as truth, focusing lovingly on the health of the community rather than obsessively on the corruptions of public life. The dangers to be avoided are cynicism and naïveté — two aspects, I think, of the same problem. Both are strategies of avoidance, and neither contributes to healthy common life.

I say these things that may seem obvious because of the number of times I have heard even thoughtful adults conclude, "I'm just not interested in politics"; "There's just not much I can do"; "It's just too depressing to think about."

This last, I believe, we can have some compassion for. It troubles me to deliver the "bad news" about American history, public life, and myths of legitimation to young people who are increasingly disheartened as simple truths appear much more ambiguous and complex than they had counted on. I don't want to take them to the edge of the existential abyss. But if we do not speak about hard things in the classroom and from the pulpit, where will the leadership come from to help each other distinguish truth from lies?

We who have the floor in those forums and others have an obligation to protest manipulation and lies in all their highly sophisticated forms. This means, most simply, to demand definitions, specific language, clarifications; to create occasions for authentic debate or, more usefully, for authentic conversation; to learn methods of nonviolent communication, use them, and teach them. And, once we have identified the lies, to turn off the TV, stop the subscription, and discredit them. We need to protect the truths we believe we can trust as such, always willing to consider more evidence, but remembering as we listen to the claims in all the clamor that, as Elizabeth O'Connor has pointed out, if a glimpse of truth is "to introduce change in us, we must stay awake and guard it from being choked out by lies."[3]

Finally, an appropriate response to the competing claims of public voices is to take these obligations quite personally. We have been "called by name" — not every one of us to public speaking, political activism in streets

3. Elizabeth O'Connor, *The Search for Silence* (Waco, Tex.: Word Books, 1972), p. 40.

and on telephones, or investigative journalism, but all of us to seek truth and follow after it, to do justice, to love mercy, and to walk humbly with God. Caring for the words we speak and testing the words we hear serve each of those ends directly.

Read Well

Learning to read is a lifelong process. What we learned in first grade or fifth, or in our first encounter with Steinbeck or Spenser or the *New York Times,* has layered and refined our reading sensibilities and strategies. If we continue to seek out worthwhile writers, we find that each one of them has something to teach us about how to read. As we make our way through the world of print, we develop criteria of value and questions that equip us to read critically and openheartedly, receptively and resistantly. I want to consider a few reading strategies that can help to serve our deepest purposes as stewards of language, story, and Scripture. Because one of the most important ways to be a good steward is to read well.

Undergraduate educators hear a lot about helping students develop "critical reading skills," which I take to mean the capacity to recognize rhetorical devices and their effects, the logic of metaphors, the structure of an argument, irony, satire, and sentimentality. I think my job as a professor of English, in which I am specifically charged with helping others receive the gifts available in literary traditions, is to help students expand the repertoire of questions they bring to the texts they read. Those questions can come from a lot of different angles. Literary study is unabashedly parasitic in the ways it borrows its questions, methods, and tools from other disciplines.

In addition to questions about form, structure, rhetoric, and imagery that focus on the stuff of which stories, poems, and plays are made, for instance, we import questions from history and the social sciences in an attempt to understand literary texts as responses to particular social and political forces in a particular historical period. We import questions from psychology that help us to see literary works in light of the psychological dynamics they embody and illustrate: the tendency to return to fundamental mythic patterns of behavior and thought, displacement, repression, substitution, wish fulfillment, individuation, and compensation. We import questions from science to understand how scientific ideas and methods may be appropriated as metaphor and structuring principles in literary texts; how literature elaborates the impact of particular scientific discoveries, mythologizes or demythologizes science and scientists, and challenges the hegemony of scientific method. We import metaphors from other art forms to give us new ways of understanding how writers work with words: how a story is an architectural form whose spaces we enter and

inhabit; how the lines of a poem are like the choreo-
graphic notation that teaches us a dance; how Crane's
work borrowed from the French Impressionists and
Hemingway's from Cézanne.

We also import questions from theology in an attempt to understand the rich and complex relations between literature and religion as repositories of insight,
symbol, mythic structures, and ways of telling truth; the
ways in which a literary work commands "belief" or "sus-
pension of disbelief"; the way it points to the Bible and
other seminal texts, and ways in which those texts have
provided categories and types that recur throughout the
culture; the ways in which stories raise and address fundamental religious questions — questions of readerly
and writerly authority and the sources of authority; the
ways in which the writer's function may be analogous to
that of priest or prophet as mediator, spokesperson, or
agent of enlightenment.

This whole range of questions leads us finally back to
words and meaning — to the ways meaning shifts according to context, to the ways words are appropriated
and sometimes co-opted by particular disciplines, to the
peculiarities of disciplinary discourse that can sometimes be so arcane as to barricade outsiders from participation. Then there are questions that good readers need
to raise that cut closer to the bone — questions that
come from a sense that the words we depend on are, indeed, as one rabbi put it, "our very life."

I've come to believe that good reading is not possible without investment of the whole self. If this is what is given us to do — to be readers, writers, and speakers — then to "do it with our whole might," in William Robinson Clark's phrase, means doing it with all our faculties — mind, heart, and gut. To read well is to enter into living relationship with another whole self. Even the most insufferable pedant comes to his or her work as a whole human being with investments, passions, defenses, and desires. As we read, we do well to remember the "who" behind the "what." If we maintain that focus, dimensions of reading open up that don't get much press in classrooms.

Consider, for instance, how good reading involves attitudes and predispositions: consent, permission, forgiveness, relinquishment, empathy, resistance, compromise. What do you have to forgive Hemingway to get the gift that he offers? His machismo? His anti-Semitism? What do you need to consent to in order to read *The Sound and the Fury* on its terms? To let go of your usual strategies of sense-making so you can enter the mind of a thirty-three-year-old idiot? To see an obnoxious, hateful, bitter man in terms of his pain? To recognize the nobility that has arisen out of oppression your own people have inflicted? What assumptions or expectations do you need to release in order to get anything at all out of *Finnegan's Wake*? Some notion of what a story is? Dependence on the conventions of continuity, plot, and character? What

68

do you have to resist in order to maintain an appropriate critical or aesthetic distance on *Lolita*? Or on *Johnny Got His Gun*?

There are three very basic questions I like to ask students as they embark on a new novel. What does this work invite you to do? What does it require of you? What does it not let you do? Because the nature of literary engagement is not, finally, detached. We will be addressed and changed, if we read well. We will be challenged and confronted and convicted and offended, bothered, unsettled, and sometimes bored — and even boredom has its uses as preparation for a deeper level of engagement — though more often it's a sign of sloth.

All this is to say that the act of reading itself is not only intellectually and emotionally engaging, but morally consequential. How we choose to read, how we submit to or question or resist the terms set by the writer, are choices that shape the habits of our minds and the habits of our hearts. Those habits determine the degree to which we are open to truth in its various guises, and capable of discerning the difference between the ring of truth and the metallic clang of lies.

Over the past few years, since I began teaching a course called "Contemplative Reading," I have found that the ancient Benedictine discipline of *lectio divina* offers an approach to many texts that may allow us to harvest their gifts in a way that frees us from what may have become deadening in classrooms, institutional schedules, and syllabi. *Lectio,* above all other approaches to reading I know, teaches us to take words personally.

In *lectio,* which Benedictines practice in the daily reading of Scripture, you read the text slowly, listening for a word or phrase that speaks to you with particular emphasis. Then you re-read the passage, allowing the key word or phrase to be a point of contact, considering how it addresses the particular circumstances of your life. On a third reading you meditate on the text and on the words it has brought to your attention as gifts peculiar to the moment, considering what response it invites. Finally, on a fourth reading you rest in words as you hear them once more. As a devotional practice, *lectio* is reserved for sacred texts and sacred time. I recommend it on those terms to anyone seeking nourishment from sacred reading.

On the other hand, what *lectio* can teach us about how to read responsibly, receptively, and fruitfully need not be reserved only for the reading of sacred texts. Poems, stories, personal memoirs, even news analysis and feature articles can be read with the prayer that in them we may be personally addressed and from them receive what Kenneth Burke calls "equipment for living." I have begun to tell my students — many of them victims of twelve years of schooling in which many have learned to resent ten-pound anthologies with unimaginative study guides and the overburdened teachers who ask plodding content questions — to "take it personally." Not simply to find what they can (to use their favorite verb) "relate to," but rather to read with an eye and ear out for words, images, scenes, sentences, and rhythms that evoke a felt response. To put a check in the margin when they are bothered or amused or offended or delighted or simply when something makes them think "Hmm." And then to go back to those places and ask what happened there. What associations were triggered? What reactions might they take time to articulate? What part of their comfort zone was invaded? To listen for direct address is to listen for an invitation and to make ready to receive precisely the gift one needs in precisely this moment of reading. On this particular reading of *Moby-Dick* it may lurk in the chapter on the whiteness of the whale. Next time, though, it may be in the little colloquy on Ahab's pipe — a three-paragraph chapter that one of my students decided was "the key chapter in *Moby-Dick*."

Not only do I think that good readers approach reading as a many-leveled, holistic, and even intimate relational act; I believe reading well involves the body as well as mind and spirit, so let me get visceral about what it means to read well by exploring three ancient metaphors for reading that deserve to be retrieved: entering the text, eating the text, and breathing the text. Each of these metaphors can open us to a dimension of engagement with words and story that enables us, as my students like to say, to "go deep," and to surface with unexpected treasures.

Let's consider texts as spaces we enter. In a very large sense, we inhabit language all the time. In it, in more than a figurative way, we live and move and have our being. And when we speak of reading, we often speak in spatial, physical, corporeal terms. We "enter" the text — or, more colloquially, we "get into" it. I remember at thirteen spending three straight days curled up in a chair with a convenient case of tonsillitis, inside the antebellum world of *Gone with the Wind,* lost to suburban southern California, deaf to my mother's inquiries about soup and aspirin. Probably many of us remember our first journey through Middle-earth and the particular, personal experience of entering the Elven forests, the caves of Moria, or the comforts of Rivendell. It's good to hang onto memories like this. The conditions of professional life afford precious few opportunities to step through the looking glass.

"Entering," a spatial metaphor, emphasizes the invitational dimension of word, poetry, or story. When we enter a story, we leave something behind. We suspend disbelief, abandon the social contract that normally binds us and adopt a new one. We consent to the terms of the story, navigate its spaces — architectural or agricultural — follow its pathways, peer through the windows it opens, and sometimes run into its walls. On occasion we lose ourselves or our bearings. We look for landmarks. We receive the writer's hospitality — or feel the discomfort of finding ourselves aliens. We enter Narnia or Purgatory or the House of Usher not only as imaginative spaces or settings, but as space-time frameworks where we actually spend a portion of our real lives. And these journeys are consequential — some every bit as consequential as actual travels to real places.

At the beginning of *The Scarlet Letter,* Hawthorne's coy and somewhat disingenuous narrator, who always has one foot outside the narrative frame, speaks of the rosebush by the prison door. "Finding it so directly on the threshold of our narrative," he says, "which is now about to issue from that inauspicious portal, we could hardly do otherwise than pluck one of its flowers and present it to the reader."[1] Well. Here's a little logical maze worthy of postmodern attention. For my purpose at present, I want to call to your attention the way the narrator points us to the threshold — a word that designates both the prison doorway and the beginning of the story — and to what is about to cross it: "the narrative," which is, as it happens, Hester Prynne herself. We ourselves are standing on a threshold, and Hester is herself the story. The curious and clever slippage of categories in this remarkable sentence puts its own ingenious spin on the allegorical devices we use to link story, space, and experience. The sentence serves as a warning, not necessarily to "abandon all hope, ye who enter here," but at least to recognize that

1. Nathaniel Hawthorne, *The Scarlet Letter* (New York: Vintage Books, Library of America edition, 1990), p. 45.

while there may be "some sweet moral blossom to be found along the track" that will take us across a threshold into a new place, we will find ourselves in something very like the proverbial dark wood as we make our way through this "tale of human frailty and sorrow."[2]

I cite this example because the spatial metaphor is so explicit. But clearly a beginning is always a point of entry, and the opening words of a story or poem or passage, a portal. Along the way, a single word can open a door. If you're reading slowly, listening to be addressed, one word or another will summon you. Those are the places where instead of going on, you go in. You pause. You do that countercultural thing you can't do at the movies: you stop. You go into a zone. You let associations come up. You watch the dots connect and a constellation of meaning and message occur in ways that are often subtle, intuitive, and hard to track, whose character is that of gift or epiphany. And you may become aware of sentences as pathways, paragraphs as labyrinths where (if you're reading Poe or Duras or Borges) you try out possibilities, run into walls, backtrack, and re-orient.

The term "interpretive horizon" is helpful in describing what happens when we read the opening sentences of a story or lines of a poem. It refers to the sense of the whole — what we can "see" or imagine from where we stand at the "threshold" of the narrative. The opening

2. Hawthorne, *The Scarlet Letter,* p. 45.

sentence gives us a place to stand. At the end of it, we already know something. Think, for instance, of one of the most famous opening sentences in American literature: "Call me Ishmael." That curious invitation situates us in a relationship, in a tradition, in a mood. The name is resonant with biblical reference, antiquity, and suggestion. "Call me . . ." introduces some uncertainty as to the actual identity of the speaker. The sentence is an imperative — even, perhaps, imperious. We find ourselves in the presence of a speaker whose self-disclosure seems reluctant, who has something to hide, but who also has and exercises authority. From this uneasy situation, we begin the complex process of constructing possibilities and making assumptions. Space and time are indeterminate, and continue to be so as the next sentence begins: "Some years ago, never mind how long . . ." But we have begun a journey and, like Dante following Virgil, we enter a narrative that takes us on a meandering and monumental journey. At each juncture of that journey, we are engaged in the process of "schema and correction," imagining the whole, given the horizon visible from our present vantage point, and correcting our assumptions — getting a sense of "where" we are — a delicate process of give-and-take between narrator and reader. We may even be teased into making assumptions we will be forced later to retract by a narrator who is, like so many of his kind, a trickster.

My point here is about entry. At the point of entry, as we begin a narrative, something opens up, and something closes behind us. And so we become vulnerable to the narrator as guide, whose promise of disclosure, insight, or surprise lures us into what might be a trap. If we're reading *Moby-Dick*, it is indeed a trap of a kind: Melville entices us into his own epistemological and theological vortex and will not let us go until we have found blessing in the darkness. At least that's my reading of *Moby-Dick*. We enter the text variously equipped. We carry with us our assumptions about story, about the truth claims of fiction, about the reliability of words, about how to distinguish the literal from the symbolic, about the stature of the text and the author's authority. And we come as we are by temperament and training: gullible, critical, seeking, resisting, watchful, playful, receptive, inquisitive. The path of our journey may be predetermined, but at every turn in a narrative, new doors stand halfway open, and we may or may not choose to go through them. Our decisions at these doors of reflection are what give us the power to be "creative readers." We can pause anywhere and follow a thought, an association, risk losing the thread as we spelunk into a sudden tunnel, make connections we weren't invited to make, probe at the secrets of the book like detectives. Because if Thoreau was right in his claim that "There are more secrets in my trade than in any other," then our task is to penetrate, investigate, even invade.

Let me return for a moment to the question of what a story requires of us. Always when we begin, we take a risk.

We assign trust upon incomplete evidence, we suspend disbelief for the moment, we quite literally make ourselves and our structures of meaning vulnerable to change. We decide to trust even someone like Huck Finn, who tells us in his shamelessly confessional manner that the book in which he last appeared was "made by Mr. Mark Twain, and he told the truth, mainly. There was things which he stretched, but mainly he told the truth." Or Dostoyevsky's unsettling narrator, who plunges into his story with this complaint: "I am a sick man. . . . I am a spiteful man. I am an unattractive man. I believe my liver is diseased." After this he goes on to comment on his self-introduction: "(A poor jest, but I will not scratch it out. I wrote it thinking it would sound very witty; but now that I have seen myself that I only wanted to show off in a despicable way, I will not scratch it out on purpose!)"[3] These are just two of many unreliable narrators who lurk, laughing up their sleeves, along the pathways of the literary landscape. With prophetic fingers in the air, they remind us that every tale we hear is mediated by a teller whose identity and purposes are partly veiled, whose disclosures may be deceptions, and whose gifts can be received only if we're willing to leave home ground and follow them on faith into what may turn out to be the "heart of darkness."

We may, on the other hand, be led into hospitable do-

3. Fyodor Dostoyevsky, *Notes from Underground* (New York: Vintage Books, reprint edition, 1994), p. 1.

mestic space. In Edith Wharton's *Age of Innocence,* every chapter opens with an elaborate description of a house — as though we need a floor plan in order adequately to understand the character who inhabits the house. "Where" precedes "who." Every item in the house is laden with significance, and gradually we become aware of the ways in which the material world described is to be understood semiotically: every thing in it is charged with value and encoded meanings. We also become aware that each chapter is a space to enter — that the structure of the book itself is highly architectural, and that we are led gradually from public social spaces to the intimate, private spaces in which key encounters occur and in which intimate discourse is permitted.

These are quite specific literary examples. But they point to the fact that we inhabit narratives — that every story provides a space in which author and reader meet. And some readers — trained readers, good readers, those who are called to teach reading — become the guides or docents in those spaces. They show people around. They help us to feel at home. They help us not to feel afraid. In that sense, good reading is a pastoral calling.

Ultimately the metaphor of entry reminds us that, as Gaston Bachelard points out, "There is no such thing as neutral space."[4] We live within multiple frames of refer-

4. Gaston Bachelard, *The Poetics of Space,* trans. Maria Jolas (Boston: Beacon Press, 1964), p. 3.

78

ence whose complex architecture shelters us from unbearable cosmic truths, but these must periodically be
torn down and remodeled to accommodate new insights
that change our assumptions. Once we have dwelt in a
particular house of fiction, we hold within us a memory
of the landscapes and intimate spaces it affords. And that
memory furnishes and redesigns our interior spaces
where thought is born and nurtured.

There are other, equally valuable metaphors for reading
that may help us reflect on the nature of our engagement
with words and text in quite different but equally sugges-
tive and useful ways. The idea of "eating" the text has a
long and curious history. As with the notion of "entering"
a text, the idea that we "eat" what we read finds its way
into our most common expressions. We struggle to "take
in" the whole argument with all its complexities. We feel
"nourished" by particular poems, "fed" by passages of
Scripture, and find there are images and ideas we need to
"chew on" for a while.

One of the most startling uses of the metaphor occurs
in Chapter 3 of Ezekiel:

> He said to me, O mortal, eat what is offered to you; eat
> this scroll, and go, speak to the house of Israel. So I
> opened my mouth, and he gave me the scroll to eat.
> He said to me, Mortal, eat this scroll that I give you
> and fill your stomach with it. Then I ate it; and in my

79

mouth it was as sweet as honey. He said to me: Mortal, go to the house of Israel and speak my very words to them. (vv. 1-4)

The intimacy of the act of eating is attested to in the sacrament of the Lord's Supper. To take the elements into our physical bodies signifies in a stark and almost scandalous way how utterly immediate, intimate, self-giving, humble, and total is the way God meets us, enters us, and dwells in us, becoming in a radical sense flesh of our flesh. So to "eat" God's Word is, similarly, to take what is sacred into our mortal selves as a source of life and a connection to the divine. We are quite literally nourished by it: "One does not live by bread alone, but by every word that comes from the mouth of the LORD" (Deut. 8:3).

These are deep spiritual truths, but they also have their application in the wide sphere of secular discourse. A literate person ingests reality — takes it in — and in digesting it, sorts out what he or she needs and does not need. In reading one learns to be an omnivore, devouring every kind and substance and shape of idea, but one also learns over time what nourishes and what sickens and kills. As Barry Sanders puts it, "Learning to read and write is metaphoric activity: a person *ingests* the shape of literacy and so gets shaped by it. Letters offer the soul its most nourishing food." And he elaborates the point: "Reading and writing generate an interior, where an active and sometimes contemplative life goes on, carried out through those essential elements that constitute the modern human being: a memory, a conscience, and a self."[5] What we eat becomes us. And just as surely, so does what we read.

This claim was perhaps more visibly true in generations when learning texts by heart was standard practice. Most of us now, due to lack of time and new pedagogical orthodoxies, learn much less by heart, and so do not "take in" what we read in the same way as people did when lessons were recited. This change, though it has its rationale, entails loss. George Steiner makes this observation about the now less common practice of rote memorization:

> To learn by heart is to afford the text or music an indwelling clarity and life-force. Ben Jonson's term, "ingestion," is precisely right. What we know by heart becomes an agency in our consciousness, a "pace-maker" in the growth and vital complication of our identity. . . . Accurate recollection and resort in remembrance not only deepen our grasp of the work: they generate a shaping reciprocity between ourselves and that which the heart knows.[6]

What we take into our memories and imaginations shapes us, alters the rhythms of breathing, speech, and

5. Barry Sanders, *A Is for Ox* (New York: Pantheon Books, 1994), p. 183, p. 70.

6. George Steiner, *Real Presences* (Chicago: University of Chicago Press, reprint edition, 1991), p. 9.

heartbeat, affects in subtle and not-so-subtle ways the very life of the body. The psalmist's exclamation "How sweet are your words to my taste, sweeter than honey to my mouth!" (119:103) invokes a metaphor so palpable, it assumes literal truth. We taste, and see that the Lord is good. The words that come to comfort in need or inspire in the breathless dark are food and drink indeed.

This brings us back to the analogy between verbal practices and the practices involved in growing and eating food. The proliferation of junk food and junk texts are similarly destructive. They erode the health of people who cannot or will not train their tastes to what body and soul rely upon for life. Eric Schlosser's *Fast Food Nation* and Morgan Spurlock's recent documentary, *Super Size Me,* testify that treating food merely as a commodity has pervasive effects on health, agriculture, the lives of the working poor, and intellectual livelihood. Both works show in painful detail how the abuse of food in unsustainable agricultural practices, cheap and dangerous processing, and deceptive marketing leads directly to widespread sickness and depression. In precisely the same way, publishing enterprises that mass-market drivel turn words into poison and deplete the appetite for healthy discourse. A steady diet of drivel weakens us. As Steiner puts it, "There is little 'ingestion'; it is the 'digest' that prevails."[7]

7. Steiner, *Real Presences,* p. 24.

Barry Sanders makes a similar distinction between ingestion and consumption: "Encountered in easy resort to electronic media of representation, much of music and of literature remains purely external. The distinction is that between 'consumption' and 'ingestion.'"[8] The music we buy and hear on a CD may touch us and even enter us, but what we play on an instrument or sing with our own voices we create out of the energies nourished and directed by something like love. We give life to the sounds we make with our bodies. In a similar way, the words we hear, learn by heart, and utter feed us and others.

So let me suggest that part of our mission is to "eat well," that we may model good health we hope for in the community. That we savor and linger over words; that we taste with delight and take in slowly. That we read, share, and memorize Scripture, poetry, and song. Memorization — words taken in, digested, and carried by our very cells — may be a more powerful tool against word erosion than any other single practice. Maybe we need a slow-language movement like the slow-food movement that would encourage us to "cook" and "eat" and "digest" the sentences we share with one another.

Most of us don't breathe any more healthily than we eat. Anyone who has been to yoga classes, studied singing,

8. Sanders, *A Is for Ox,* p. 10.

or practiced meditation has had the experience of attending to breath, and perhaps finding how poorly we tend to breathe. Many of us literally conduct our lives at a breathless pace, so the breath of life cannot fill us and enliven us. When we don't breathe, we can't speak. Sentences are mumbled and swallowed. Words are gifts withheld.

I remember a student I had some years ago who spoke so softly and hesitantly, and so breathlessly, that no one in class could hear her. When I would ask her to speak up, she would gamely start in again, still at a volume impossible to hear at a distance of more than ten feet. Whatever inhibition kept in this breathless, tentative state deprived the rest of us of intelligence I knew she had to offer. The kind of speaking that imparts a gift is impossible without breathing. So the third metaphor I want to reflect on with you is "breathing" the text.

The Japanese haiku poets understand perhaps as fully as anyone on earth the significance of inbreath and outbreath in poesis. A haiku poem is a breath poem that can be uttered in a single outbreath. It is a long outbreath — seventeen syllables, more or less. A long, slow, deep inbreath is needed to fuel the poem, and then:

An hour's snow —
Heaven and earth briefly settle
All their old differences.

The green of pine trees
Never tires my eyes
So, too, the face of my friend.[9]

To utter these poems properly, one has to breathe deeply and release slowly — instructions any yoga or meditation teacher will give as prerequisite to relaxing into the work to be done. The poem itself is a teacher. Light as a breath, it alights in the mind and opens a space of quiet around it. These two poems, like many haiku, harbor a little gentle humor, so the breath it takes to utter them may end in a final release of laughter.

The Japanese are masters of this form. But in English poetry as well, metrics, the study of poetic rhythms and cadences, can teach us to breathe text as song. Every breath space — period, comma, line break — allows a silence in which words just spoken may echo and resonate. We learn this most easily in song; but what we learn from song can be applied to the way we read and speak a sentence, making it available for hearers in a way that gives it full weight. As we read a text aloud, we literally breathe life into it. Steiner observes that "The meanings of poetry and the music of those meanings, which we call metrics, are also of the human body. The echoes of sensibility which they elicit are visceral and

9. James Luguri, *To Make a World: One Hundred Haiku and One Waka* (Peter Luguri, 1987), p. 76.

tactile."[10] Which is to say that breathing the text actually confers a dimension of meaning. Phrase by phrase, pause by pause, we open small silences in which to take in the words. They need those silences to grow in. Meditative practices like breath prayer and centering prayer, as well as *lectio divina,* can inform our lives as readers and slow us into deeper receptivity. When we hear the voice of the psalmist singing "Whatever has life and breath, praise the Lord!" (Ps. 150:6), we might consider how breathing itself may be a form of thanksgiving — receiving and releasing what the Lord gives and takes away. So all the words we utter have their roots in prayer and enter our minds and hearts by inspiration.

Our lives are lived in relationship to words, written and spoken, sacred and mundane. They are manna for the journey. As embodied beings we take our whole bodies with us into the act of reading, which, at its best, is spacious, full-bodied, wholehearted, and infused with the breath of life.

10. Steiner, *Real Presences,* p. 9.

Stay in Conversation

S everal years ago a friend and I devised and taught an experimental course titled "Conversational English for Native Speakers." It was a missionary enterprise. Our objective was to help the young and the media-impaired rediscover the delights of exchanging words, and, in a larger sense, to help equip them to cherish and steward the gift of language. Along with passages from a few contemporary linguists and essayists, we had them read Jane Austen for the rich, lively, courteous, confrontational, articulate conversations her novels offer as models of what was once politely called social intercourse. Anyone who harbors the notion that Austen's circumscribed world of rural English parlors and parks was small-minded, provincial, or dull needs to reread *Pride and Prejudice* to reencounter the vigor of Elizabeth Bennett's quick wit and astute social observation, or the generosity of Jane's moral reflection, or the instructive trajectory of Darcy's growth in self-knowledge, largely through defining moments of honest conversation with the woman he comes to love. In that novel, as in others that predate the entertainment industry (and so remind us that talking to one another was once a primary form of shared entertainment), we may retrieve some vision of the gifts available in good conversation.

Conversation is not simple. Good conversation is rare. We do not live in a culture in which the art of conversation is widely cultivated. It is hard to resist slipping into the scripts and formulas marketed by popular television and talk radio and to maintain the kind of sustained conversation that enlarges thought and nourishes the spirit. Barry Sanders, in a discussion of the effects of electronically mediated language learning, concludes that all the thousands of hours of viewing and hearing language "does not add up to orality. Anyone who speaks through electronic media has had his or her patter carefully shaped by a script; the delivery — tone, intonation, emphasis — has been rehearsed." He adds, "TV kills the human voice. People cannot argue with anything on the screen. TV images pass by too fast for young minds to consider or analyze them."[1] No matter how "lively" the conversation modeled on television, the medium itself works to suppress the spontaneity, imagination, and attentive listening required in actual conversation.

What passes for conversation is often a predictable

1. Barry Sanders, *A Is for Ox* (New York: Pantheon Books, 1994), p. 38.

recitation of undeveloped thoughts and unexamined feelings, exchanged as the currency that buys rudimentary comfort and affirmation: "Know what I mean?" "Yeah." This kind of two-stroke exchange, just a notch above grunting at each other — what a friend of mine wryly called "grooming behavior" — is hardly an evil in itself. Some of it may be necessary. But neither is it sufficient for sustaining intellectual vitality or fostering authentic intimacy. Conversation confined to such formulaic exchanges may simply serve as a narcotic to dull the hunger pangs of an undernourished spirit.

To "converse" originally meant to live among or together, or to act together, to foster community, to commune with. It was a large verb that implied public, cooperative, and deliberate action. When we converse, we act together toward a common end, and we act upon one another. Indeed, conversation is a form of activism — a political enterprise in the largest and oldest sense — a way of building and sustaining community. Consider, for instance, the large, long public conversations out of which have emerged the very structures and foundational documents that give shape to the social contracts we live by. A good conversationalist directs attention, inspires, corrects, affirms, and empowers others. It is a demanding vocation that involves attentiveness, skilled listening, awareness of one's own interpretive frames, and a will to understand and discern what is true. It may be that we don't often enough consider conversation as a form of social action, as a ministry, or as a spiritual discipline. That it may be all three, and that it is a significant part of our life and calling as people of faith, may be more evident if we consider what good conversation does.

In a broad and true sense, good conversation is life-giving: it inspires and invigorates. Talking with students once about the qualities of good prose- writing, I put a series of descriptors on the board and asked them to choose those that best expressed what they hoped for in their own writing: *precise, clear, accurate, clever, graceful, witty, powerful, memorable, economical, amusing, persuasive, lively.* One student, for whom English was a second language, lit up at the word *lively.* "That's it," he exclaimed before anyone else had spoken. "I want my words to be lively." So we talked for a while about what that might mean, and why liveliness in our use of language, both oral and written, matters: how lively language is life-giving — how it may literally, physiologically, quicken our breath, evoke our laughter, raise our eyebrows, open our hearts, renew our energies. Lively language invents and evokes and sustains.

One of the liveliest conversationalists I have known, a woman rich in experience who held her own opinions vigorously and was curious about those of others, enjoyed and imparted a gift of seeing the ordinary as story or drama. She had a high respect for amusement. Walking the streets of San Francisco with her was an exercise in improvisational observation and comment. Suddenly, gestures, accents, angles of hats, funny walks, and the dissonance of urban sounds became material for reflection, as though everything we encountered were an invitation. And so it is.

To see that way, to respond to what meets the eye with question, comment, and counterpoint, is to receive and give life at every turn. "Look at that," she'd say of a line in the post office. "Those old people need benches to sit on. That man with the cane is going to be there for fifteen minutes. How much would it cost the city to provide a few benches and hand out numbers?" (She wrote letters to public officials about such things.) Or "Those women are going to get the best vegetables in the bin! Look at the way they drive those shopping carts! They're in here for competitive sport!"

It may not be that all the world is a stage for most of us the way it was for my friend, but being with her taught me something about the lively art of comment. Whether critical, amused, curious, reminiscent, or reflective, her practice of bringing language to what she saw imparted density and richness to ordinary experience. It brought the merest events of daily life into sharper focus and enabled me to see them as invitational and thought-provoking. That is how I have come to understand the quality of "liveliness," and what I have learned to hope for in conversation — that it sharpens what might tend toward dullness, that it throws into relief what might tend to seem flat, that it reckons with cause and process where one might otherwise simply register an inert object, and that, in doing these things, it imparts a breath of life, drawn from the source.

Conversation, like good reading, nourishes. The universal coupling of meals with conversation suggests the deep consonance that links those activities. In conversation we feed and are fed by one another. Replacing dinner table conversation with electronic entertainment has left many literally starved for nourishing words.

Such nurture takes time. One way to minister to a busy and hurried people is to take, and offer, time for conversation — not the quick news update or five-minute check-in, but the exploratory, reflective, expansive kind of conversation one might have had more regularly over tea or on the verandah on summer evenings or by the fireside on winter evenings in a more leisurely time. (The leisure required has always to some extent been class-bound, but there is good evidence in what historians can retrieve of oral culture that even the laboring classes have, except under very oppressive conditions, cultivated the lively art of conversation at wells and over handwork and while walking to and from fields.) Josef Pieper makes the strongest possible argument for the importance of leisure in his now-classic work, *Leisure: The Basis of Culture,* when he writes, "Culture depends for its very existence on leisure, and leisure, in its turn, is not possible unless it has a durable and consequently living link with a church community and with divine worship."[2] It is no mere nostalgia to recognize that our capacity to sustain and enjoy good conversation has been seriously diminished by the proliferation of other forms of entertainment, and by work lives that leave us enervated by long commutes and rapid-fire electronic communication, that often forestalls face-to-face conversation in real time and real presence.

A youth pastor I know, recognizing a particular hunger among teenagers whose instant messaging, cell phones, and e-mail filled their lives with unsatisfying facsimiles of conversation, scheduled regular "coffee dates" and walks with them one by one, simply to engage them in conversation about anything that mattered to them. She knew the power of generous listening, of asking the next question. She asked them, in effect, Who are you? What is it like to be living your particular life? How do you cope with your own sufferings? How do you feel about the challenges you encounter in the world you're inheriting? Why have you made the particular choices you've made thus far? What delights you? What makes you afraid? What may we offer one another at this stage in our journeys?

This kindly endeavor offers a promising model for an increasingly needful form of ministry. It may be that we

---

2. Josef Pieper, Preface, *Leisure: The Basis of Culture*, www.new-jerusalem.com/pieper.htm.

who are in the church, to be what we are called to be, must become increasingly intentional about providing occasions for leisurely conversations that take us beyond the enforced superficialities of hurried contact. If it is true, as I have read, that over 60 percent of Americans don't even gather once a day with their families or housemates over a meal, that statistic alone may give us some measure of what has been lost and incentive to imagine how it might be retrieved.

Not only the words exchanged but the settings that promote conversation deserve attention. The ceremonies of afternoon tea or weekly "calls" upon neighbors may be irretrievable (though the English department I inhabit, thanks to a dedicated secretary, actually gathers for tea and talk once a week), but the element of ceremony deserves not to be overlooked. The ritual character of such meetings sets them apart from the busyness that serves production and profit, and from the ad hoc encounters that take place in the midst of our multitasking. Sites like bars with intrusive background music (and often wall-mounted televisions) have become venues in which young adults commonly engage in what might be some of the most determinative conversations of their lives. People "hang out" together, but in ways that seem less disposed to the kind of conversation my North Carolina grandfather meant when he invited friends to "come on in and set a spell" or my Virginia-bred grandmother when she went "vis'ting." Curiously, the word *visit* has fallen into disuse, or rather has come to mean something like "visiting" the site of a new building project or making a diplomatic "visit" to a country where negotiations are to occur. We occasionally "revisit" a decision. But visiting one another in the oldest sense of taking the time truly to look at and "see" one another, to settle into each other's presence, and to ask each other questions, offer each other stories, reflect together on our common life, and share our fears and hopes, requires a high level of intention and deliberate space-clearing. "Quality time" has become a scarce commodity for many of us, and consequently we may find ourselves at a loss as to how to use it purposefully and well when we do have it.

Using conversation purposefully can mean a variety of things. Conversation is an exchange of gifts. Native American tribal wisdom teaches that when you encounter a person on your life path, you must seek to find out what gifts you have for one another so that you may exchange them before going your separate ways. This seems true even of daily encounters with those we know well. We come into one another's presence bearing whatever harvest of experience the day has offered, and we foster relationship by making a gift of what we have received. Not everyone has the capacity I value in a good friend of mine, who can turn the simplest incident at the checkout counter or a stoplight into an amusing story, but crafting into sharable story what has happened to us is one of the tasks that relationship requires.

Storytelling, though it may be the oldest art form we have, does not come naturally. We learn the forms and shapes of narrative from the culture around us. Few of us weave "yarns" or sing ballads; folk tales come to us now mostly through well-illustrated story books marketed to children; oral culture gives way early in life to story mediated by television, film, and print. Still, the gift of story, told spontaneously face-to-face in real time, is irreplaceable. Singling out, considering, and perhaps even embellishing lived events in response to the simple query "How was your day?" transforms experience into shared pleasure. In the process of such sharing, to let one thing lead to another, to allow memories to be triggered or questions to be raised, is to allow story to work as leaven and the bread of daily life to expand.

Making experience into story is only one way to share the gifts of the day. Sometimes fruitful conversation comes from articulating questions that the day raised, decisions it exacted, dilemmas or problems it posed. Sometimes it comes from recognizing and passing on what lessons it offered. Sometimes from confessing discouragements or failures that elicit the giving and receiving of comfort that is so basic to shared life, it is even mentioned in wedding vows. "Everyone," Elizabeth O'Connor has written, "needs someone who will ask him to give an account of himself, so that he can face into his life and confess who he really is." She goes on to suggest that since liturgical confession has disappeared or become vestigial in many people's lives and religious practices, "Perhaps that meaning can be restored in conversation that is carried on in awareness that he who speaks confesses, and that those who listen are priests."[3]

Even argument may be a gift; our efforts to persuade one another, kindly undertaken, are important occasions for testing and honing the convictions we live by and challenging the commonplaces that so easily settle into prejudice or thoughtless habit. In conversation, adults teach children, and friends and lovers teach one another.

While it is easy to praise and encourage the art of good conversation, it is more difficult actually to retrieve and practice it. We call it an art because it doesn't come naturally; it requires the energy necessary to overcome the entropy of fatigue and passivity. So it may help the cause to consider singly the skills and attitudes necessary to good conversation.

Deliberation. The root idea of *deliberate* is to act with free will, care, and consciousness, weighing costs and effects. When we deliberate, we take responsibility for our choices. And conversation always entails a choice for something (community, connection, shared space, time, thought, vulnerability) and a choice against something (passivity, solitude, self-focus).

3. Elizabeth O'Connor, *The Search for Silence* (Waco, Tex.: Word Books, 1972), p. 34, p. 38.

Though the circumstances in which we enter into conversation may often be unplanned, the entering is still a decision to set other agendas aside and attend. Deliberation distinguishes conversation from "idle chatter," which requires little and offers less. When we enter seriously and intentionally into conversation, we effectively commit to thinking with the other, being responsive, listening, and caring. As in a sport, we commit to hold up our end — to hit the ball back or to pass it (depending on your favorite sports metaphor). As in a dance, we commit to learning and practicing the steps that will empower and enable participants to delight in one another. If we take the invitation seriously, even when it is spontaneous and playful, we bring appropriate will and energy to an exchange that can leave all who consent to it enriched.

Curiosity. It was Oliver Sacks who first made me reflect on curiosity as a form of compassion. An ingenious and creative neurologist now well-known for his "clinical tales," he begins his work as diagnostician and healer with the implicit question "What is it like to be you?" Starting from a focus on "who" rather than "what" frames his work in a relational, holistic way. The diagnostic process he records in the stories in *The Man Who Mistook His Wife for a Hat* is quirky, inventive, playful, and ad hoc, intently focused on helping him find out what he may need to know without predetermining what that might be. The authentic curiosity he brings to these encounters is exemplary in the respect it conveys, the attentiveness it generates, and the freedom it imparts to the patient to help determine what matters in diagnosis and treatment. Rather than confining himself to a prescriptive notion of what is medically relevant, Sacks encourages patients to offer any information about themselves that seems to them to matter, and pursues that information with complete confidence that it does matter, though he may not yet know in what way.

In one such "clinical tale," he tells how he approached a young autistic man whom others had dismissed as "an idiot" by having him draw and then scrutinizing with remarkable care and aesthetic interest his style of representation for whatever clues it might present. In the now-famous title story of *The Man Who Mistook His Wife for a Hat,* he recounts his efforts to understand the rare visual disorder of a highly intelligent patient by coming to his home, looking at his paintings, and inquiring about his reading of *Anna Karenina.* Sacks's sentences often offer several alternative verbs as he tries to get at the mysterious internal processes of this patient:

He approached these [portraits] — even of those near and dear — as if they were abstract puzzles or tests. He did not relate to them, he did not behold. No face was familiar to him, seen as a "thou," being just identified as a set of features, an "it." . . . A face, to us, is a person looking out — we see, as it were, the person through his persona, his face. But for Dr. P. there was no persona in this sense — no outward persona, and no person within.[4]

It takes Sacks several sentences to achieve the precision required to honor the mystery and complexity of what he sees in his patient — and numerous nearly synonymous verbs and adjectives — circling the observed behavior to find the precise naming that might yield diagnostic insight.

Curiosity like this is open-ended, patient, humble, and generous. It enlivens conversation between doctor and patient by freeing it, at least to a degree, from the conventions that predetermine what may be disclosed and considered. Sacks's childlike habit of mind is comparable to that of Sherlock Holmes in the old Basil Rathbone movies, where Holmes bursts into a room, looks around, spies some insignificant object, and cries, "Hello! What's this?" It is a predisposition to seek, notice, consider anything that is at all odd or unusual — to see everything as potentially meaningful. And while Holmes is famous for the meticulous logic of his reasoning, what is more striking in both those stories and in Sacks's clinical tales is the highly intuitive quality of open-ended curiosity that is willing to pursue any path.

4. Oliver Sacks, "The Man Who Mistook His Wife for a Hat," in *The Man Who Mistook His Wife for a Hat and Other Clinical Tales* (New York: Simon & Schuster/Touchstone, 1998), p. 13.

Good conversation comes from just such flexibility. As observations come up, it meanders, following a course that tends in a particular direction, but moves responsively in new directions as associations are triggered, words are paused over to consider their implications, examples are invented, connections are made. Like jazz, it is a work of improvisation that entails listening intently for what the others are doing and moving with them. The curiosity which sustains that intensity pauses at every turn to notice what's happening, to raise new questions and pursue them. In a gentle pursuit of ideas, it makes room for the unexpected. Exercised in this way, curiosity becomes an avenue of grace. Conversation pursued in this spirit is full of surprise. It connects one idea or thought or analogy with another in ways that could not have been predicted.

Raising good questions, though, takes practice. There are only six basic question words: who, what, when, where, how, and why. At any point, in any situation, any of them may be posed. But posing them, rather than rushing to easy and swift closure, means forestalling the satisfaction of closure and taking a certain risk. So much conversation grinds to a premature halt with end-game moves: "Yeah, me too." "Right." "Well, isn't that something." To ask the next question is to keep the ball in play. One must be willing to expend the energy required to keep listening, to turn the next corner, and to remain open to surprise. Insofar as conversation takes us in unplanned directions, it involves at least some slight risk that we might reveal our ignorance, look foolish, find ourselves emotionally or intellectually or verbally unprepared. So to pursue it at all is an act of trust in our own reserves, in our companions' generosity, and in the Spirit that gives us, if we listen, the words we need.

Listening. The difference between hearing and listening is significant. Some years ago I attended a conference at which the brilliant and opinionated psychologist Bruno Bettelheim addressed clinicians and educators about the nature of healing encounter. Early in the first session, he asked the audience what they thought was the main work of the clinician. One ready reply was "Just to listen." "Just listen?!" Bettelheim boomed in return, somewhat contemptuously. "My dog can just listen." Listening is only helpful, he went on to explain, if it is skilled, focused, and responsive. The "just" that suggests it is a simple matter belies the complexity of listening well. Listening well means knowing when to interject questions, when to redirect the conversation, and, more importantly, in what terms to interpret the other's narrative. It means recognizing that the speaker is making purposeful choices, consciously or unconsciously, and considering what those purposes might be. It means accepting the tension between making judgments and withholding judgment as the other's story or line of reasoning unfolds. It means hearing and noting the omissions. And it means listening not only *through* the words spoken, but *to* them.

The best listeners I know pause over words. "That's an interesting way of putting it," they muse, or they ask, "What exactly do you mean by that?" The consciousness that every word is a choice, that each word has its own resonance, nuance, emotional coloring, and weight informs their sense of what is being communicated. This kind of listening comes close to what we engage in when we listen to music. The shape of sentences, the enunciation and emphasis, the images and metaphors, the idioms all give a particular character to the thoughts being expressed — sometimes, indeed, complicate or modify or even belie them. So if we are to listen well, we must learn to listen for the "how" and "why" as well as the "what." A good listener loves words, respects them, pays attention to them, and recognizes vague approximations as a kind of falsehood. The standard to which Twain holds writers isn't altogether unreasonable as a standard for good conversation. This care for responsible use of words might be compared to keeping one's instrument in tune so that the melody may be played truly.

Honesty. That kind of truth is as important as factual accuracy. What "rings true," what passes the test of emotional as well as cognitive or historical accuracy, matters in all of our exchanges. Good conversation serves the truth. It clarifies and nuances. It corrects and refines. To be in conversation is, ideally, to be seeking a deeper or more comprehensive grasp of some truth by means of dialogue, so that it proceeds on the assumption that no one of us is at any point (courtroom oaths notwithstanding) in possession of the "whole truth," but rather that each of us may bring a perspective to bear that may complement and modify the perspective of others. The willingness to change one's mind in the course of conversation or civil argument seems, alas, to be a rare quality. It is much more common to enter and leave conversations hanging on to our own convictions and constructions, unchanged but for the momentary satisfaction of having "had our say."

I know a few remarkable individuals with sufficient humility and confidence to open themselves to persuasion in conversation; to talk with them is exhilarating because of the feeling they convey that something new might be permitted to happen, depending on what we say to one another. Conversation with one of my colleagues has this character. He and I often disagree. But rather than focusing on the disagreement, he spends a good deal of time gathering information, motivated by exactly the kind of the generous curiosity I recall in Sacks. "How did you come to that conclusion yourself?" he might ask. Or "I hadn't thought to put it that way; that casts the problem in a different light." Or "You frame it a little differently than I do. Why would that be?" He notices differences not only in the "content," but also in the construction of arguments and ideas, and considers what they imply so that his own understanding of what is at issue might be broadened and deepened. His willingness to listen for correction is always a lesson in humility and grace, and even in courage. Good conversation, if it is to involve mutual teaching and learning, does require courage — not only the courage of one's convictions, but also the courage to admit one's limited range of vision and to allow for change, which always exacts some cost in comfort and the security of being "right."

Both intellectual and emotional vulnerability contribute to good conversation. It's easy to make fun of the various clichéd uses of "sharing" as an enforced group activity. (My daughter's wry response to many a new situation is a smarmy imitation of the T-group directive "Share how that makes you feel," and to my occasional random opinionating, "Thank you for sharing!") But *sharing* is a lovely word, worth preserving from exclusive appropriation by pop psychologists and kindergarten curricula. Literally meaning "dividing and giving part away," sharing thoughts and feelings entails both the work of careful expression and the work of trust-building. Shared secrets, for instance, bind us in mutual trust and accountability. To share my inner thoughts with you is to invite you into protected space; it is a kind of hospitality extended and received.

Part of the giving and receiving is the inevitable rewording and translating that takes place between partners who extend themselves outside the familiar ground of their internal monologues into a more public arena where words and meanings are negotiated and nudged into new service. You may use a word differently than I do. Your thought may make sense to me only after I re-word it to myself. So if you say, "I'm annoyed about this decision," I might wonder whether your idea of annoyance falls, as mine does, on the spectrum between irritation and outrage, and I may ask, moreover, whether it is the process or the likely effect of the decision that bothers you. So in the "backing and forthing" of conversation, we shape and hone and polish each other's terms into more precise meaning.

The process can be amusing. Certainly the inevitable slippages of meaning, context, and intention that give your words a different shading from mine offer ample material for laughter. And good conversation, even the most serious, has to make room for laughter. Like the banana peel that is the stock-in-trade of slapstick, slippery words lead us headlong into puns, double meanings, and unintended suggestiveness. The stuff of which jokes are made is also the place where wit works its magic.

But the high play of witty conversation can degenerate into exhibitionistic banter if it is not tempered by an opposite and perhaps even more important virtue, which is the capacity to hold one's peace, to wait, to pause for thought, to consent to shared silence. Words need space. Witty, weighty, well-chosen words need more space than others to be received rightly, reckoned with, and responded to. That space, the silence between words, is as important a part of good conversation as rests are a part of a pleasing, coherent musical line. The silences in conversation honor and support the words they carry, as water supports the vessels that float on it. Only in silence can the "listening into" take place — the pausing over words, meanings, implications, associations — and the waiting — for the Spirit to speak, for the right response to surface. At its deepest level, good conversation holds a balance we seek in prayer between speaking and listening, waiting for the unplanned, epiphanic moment that comes unbidden in the midst of what we thought we were pursuing. Those silences also distinguish substantive conversation from idle chatter that fills all the "air time" available, often as a protection against the silences in which a new thought might take us where we're not sure we want to go. When silences are allowed, conversation can rise to the level of sacred encounter.

Legend has it that when St. Francis and St. Clare met together for conversation on a few rare occasions, the house where they met glowed like fire. Though that story sets a rather unnervingly high conversational standard, it does suggest how literally talking together may generate heat and light and spiritual energy. The voluminous records of Luther's "Table Talk," Samuel Johnson's gatherings in London pubs, Madame de Stael's and Gertrude Stein's weekly salons, the meetings of the Inklings in Oxford and the Parnassiens in Paris and the literati of the Algonquin Club in New York testify to how much creative work has its roots in conversation. More essentially than intellectual or artistic creativity, conversation is a source of the work most central to our human calling, which is to enter into relationship and love one another. Words are irreducible instruments of love; actions may at times "speak louder," but where no words are shared, relationship languishes. Words are also buffers. They line the pathway of relationship and provide the currency of negotiation.

Good conversation is a courtesy, a kindness, a form of *caritas* that has as its deepest implicit intention binding one another together in understanding and love. In this regard I remember a particularly poignant moment at a twentieth class reunion, when a man my age sat down next to me, smiled, and said by way of re-introduction, "You were the only girl in tenth-grade English who would talk with me. I've always remembered that." Though it was hardly to my great credit at the time, since I would likely have talked with anyone who sat across the aisle in that class, I was touched that such a small and ordinary act of simple connection would be so long remembered. I did remember talking with him, and that he was shy, and that something in his shyness met my own and gave me the confidence to speak.

I have observed since that a quality the best conversationalists conspicuously share is generosity. They can minister even to the most problematic partners — the inarticulate, the painfully introverted, and the indifferent. One sterling example of such generosity was a French professor who regularly sat at a dormitory lunch table where only French was to be spoken. Quite deliberately, I noticed, she chose the tables populated by students still struggling for basic mastery. Magically, she wove together shreds of sentences and picked up the dropped stitches of missing helping verbs, wrong tenses, and false cognates, working them into something resembling sprightly and civil discourse. And she had a good time doing it. The range she achieved with very little help from her table companions was remarkable: from laughter over salt mistakenly passed to serious shared concerns about Americans in Vietnam and the rising costs of tuition. I still wonder whether she ever fully realized what a gift she imparted to those who were still among the lame, the halt, and the blind as far as spoken French was concerned.

A quality she shared with others I place in her league, in addition to her pleasure in and high regard for words, was dignity. The word itself seems slightly antique these days. My own sense of its meaning includes a certain respectful distance maintained in order to allow the words exchanged the space that makes them available for reflection. What she did was quite in contrast to the "instant intimacy" so common in American public discourse and behavior: she held something of self in reserve and helped us all to maintain focus on the issue or object at hand. We considered together some shared concern rather than leaping to the "I-thou" dimension, which, too quickly entered into, can forestall and forfeit the equally important business of reasoning together about those matters external to our selves that affect us all. The metaphors of "breadth" and "depth" remind us of some balance to be maintained between conversation that equips us to navigate the world by naming and mapping and deliberating and conversation that discloses us to one another and brings us into relationship that reaffirms our common dependencies and our importance to each other. Like prayer, good conversation fashions words into vessels that carry living water.

And prayer itself is conversation. To be in conversation with God is, like tithing, a way of returning to him some part of the gift of words we have received from Him who is the Word. Like the long, intimate conversations of shared life among partners and friends, conversation with God keeps us turning toward, confiding in, trusting, and learning from the very source of life and language. In that intimate conversation we can be sure of receiving whatever direction and words we need for all the others. Jesus' promise to the disciples as he sent them forth to preach can be claimed by each one of us as we enter into our daily encounters, hoping to find lively and life-giving words: ". . . do not be anxious how you are to speak or what you are to say; for what you are to say will be given to you in that hour" (Matt. 10:19).

Share Stories

T here was a man who had two sons. There was a king who had three daughters. There was an old woman who lived deep in the forest. There was much talk and excitement in Hobbiton. A boy child born to save his people was hidden in a basket. A disobedient prophet spent three nights in the belly of a fish. A sower went out to sow. The king is dead; long live the king.

We know these stories. We recognize "Once upon a time" as an invitation to leave the confusions of daily life and enter the dream space that culture provides where there are gifts of knowledge we can't receive unless we step over the threshold into story. There, we are "equipped for living," sometimes even for survival.

A recent study conducted by the NEA called "Reading at Risk: A Survey of Literary Reading in America" shows that less than half the adult population of the United States reads literature — defined as reading at least one novel, short story, poem, or play in leisure time in the course of a year.[1] So the question remains: What do we stand to lose if the reading public reads fewer stories, poems, and plays?

Some would say what we lose is relatively insignificant. With the global crises we are facing, it may be more important to read the varieties of nonfiction that focus on the volatile social, economic, and political issues that concern us all. It may be that we'd be better equipped at the moment by reading *A People's History of the United States* or *The Shock Doctrine* or reports from the WTO conventions and their protestors, rather than Milton or Poe or Fitzgerald. I spend a good part of my own reading life these days (the shreds of it that are left after reading piles of undergraduate prose) trying to become reliably informed about resource use, militarization, and relationships between the government and the large corporations that shape our choices, if not our ends. But before bedtime, my husband and I may dip into Dostoyevsky or George Eliot or Michael Malone (a fine Southern mystery writer worth discovering if you're a mystery buff). Or he may read me a poem by Wendell Berry along with a psalm.

These moments are precious, not only because reading to one another fosters and deepens our ongoing conversation, but also because being taken into story keeps us "dwelling in possibility." We need story, poetry, play, and

1. Garrick Davis, "Reading at Risk," NEA Newsroom, 8 July 2004 (available at www.nea.gov/news/news04/ReadingAtRisk.html).

song to replenish the wellsprings of imagination, to feed the spirit, to foster compassion. Indeed, I would go so far as to claim that there are certain kinds of understanding that we have no access to except by means of story.

As Thoreau argues throughout his leisurely reflections in *Walden,* we can understand things rightly only if we understand them over time — that is, in terms of their stories of conception, growth, development, and death. Everything we look at is embedded in story. That sounds so obvious, and yet the narrative dimension of our lives is routinely subordinated to other forms of accounting — spreadsheets, flow charts, predictive instruments, statistics — presentations of information that can distract us from the subtle, even mysterious processes unique to particular times and places that can be grasped only by means of the active imagining that shapes experience into story.

If I could teach only one thing to undergraduates, it would be to "think process," which is simply a way of saying, Pay attention to the story that lies behind every product you purchase, every system you rely on, every event you witness, every person you meet. Novels and short stories invite us to reflect on several basic questions. How do things happen? How are they related? What have they to do with us? How do we make our judgments, and how are we a part of what we witness? Whose story do we inhabit, and on what terms? And for what do we take responsibility?

113

In addition to offering us narrative frames and narrative continuities, stories also offer moments of epiphany. They remind us about how those continuities are liable to be broken open at any point by surprise that comes from outside the boundaries of conventional expectations. In their poetic dimension, they offer the kind of knowing that comes in glimpses, moments, flashes of memory, associations. Good stories unfold the consequences of defining moments that can be recognized as such only in retrospect. The storytellers who have gone before us have left us a legacy of tantalizing glimpses behind the veil that can be lifted only a moment at a time.

A note from Ecclesiastes rings in all stories: there is nothing new under the sun. In 1916 Georges Polti posited the widely cited idea that there are only thirty-six plots or "dramatic situations."[2] And yet, that acknowledgment of finitude turns out not to be so bleak or limiting as it might sound. Rather than a yawn of ennui, the declaration comes to seem one of reassurance and even delighted recognition. There it is again! We know this!

Reflecting on what gifts she had to offer in her later years, an old woman I knew once said simply, "I've been through things." Characters like Lear and Dilsey and Baby Suggs and Old Jack who have been "through things" help us to

2. Georges Polti, *The Thirty-Six Dramatic Situations* (New York: Writer, 1977).

understand how richness of experience, even the most searing, blesses us in the struggle. They offer no false hope or sanguine optimism about the nobility of the human spirit or the power of positive thinking. But they do assert the possibility of dignity and of hope that is bigger than the odds, and passes understanding. To accept the invitation of good stories is to enter into deep and pleasurable reflection on very old philosophical questions: what we can know and what we must do. They widen the frames through which we watch the human spectacle and show us how wounds are windows and how even in sorrow we may find inducements to choose life.

Unlike socio-economic analysis, which attempts to provide a "bottom line" explanation, stories by definition leave room for re-readings, re-interpretations, competing stories. We can keep revisiting the story of Abraham and Isaac and retelling it because the story leaves so many unanswered questions. In *Legends of Our Time,* Elie Wiesel explains the invitation and command to revisit these stories as a matter of establishing fundamental connection and identity: "The Haggadah, with its story of the Exodus, confirmed our hope. Is it not written that each Jew must regard himself, everywhere and at all times, as having himself come out of Egypt? And that, for each generation, the miracle will be renewed?"[3] To in-

---

3. Elie Wiesel, *Legends of Our Time* (New York: Schocken Books, reprint edition, 2004), pp. 25-26.

habit Judeo-Christian tradition is to live our lives in intimate relation to a repertoire of stories that shape our hopes, our self-understanding, our notions of history, and the stories we invent, which necessarily borrow their deep structures, imagery, and language from the foundational stories that beget them. Those elements of story are a rich inheritance. Think simply of phrases, for instance, that evoke whole constellations of character, situation, and conflict, and that work like seed crystals in our memories to bring us "home" to a place of knowing:

> Take off your shoes. You are on holy ground.
> Here am I, LORD.
> But yet you have another son.
> I, alone, have survived to tell thee.
> This night will thy life be required of thee.
> This, my son, who was dead, is alive again.
> Martha, Martha, you are busy about many things.
> Son, behold your mother.

The Coptic fathers touch the cross as a way of relocating and grounding themselves in spiritual reality. To return to and "touch" the stories that have borne our truths serves a similar purpose. They locate us. Where they don't offer explanation or instruction directly, they can comfort, encourage, and remind.

But the stories that matter also complicate our lives. Good stories are always slightly precarious places to go, because even those that are deeply familiar retain the ability to surprise, challenge, and disconcert. They remind us of mysteries we have to live with and dwell in without ever arriving at conclusive or exclusive understanding. So stories keep us "negatively capable." I'd like to see negative capability listed among the virtues we urge upon the young. Tolerance for ambiguity is one of the most urgent disciplines and attitudes we can cultivate today. It is the opposite of bigotry, rigidity, and culture-bound vision. There can be no peacemaking or even effective negotiation without it.

Tribal cultures teach this. In most, the storyteller bears a heavy responsibility. A repertoire of stories binds the people together, reminds them of who they are and of the mysteries that keep them all in relationship to divine powers. Told again and again, their stories offer hope, issue warnings, give direction, guide hearers through dangers, and point toward what can't be told. Hyemeyohsts Storm, a Sioux, in his beautiful collection of stories and reflections titled *Seven Arrows,* says this about the function of stories in his tribal community:

> Stories were used among the People to Teach the meaning of the Sun Dance Way. They were themselves a Way of Understanding among the People, and also between different Peoples. Because the People did not have a written language, these Stories were memorized

and passed down in one way through countless generations.

. . . These stories are almost entirely allegorical in form, and everything in them should be read symbolically. Every story can be symbolically unfolded for you through your own Medicines, Reflections, and Seekings. As you do this, you will learn to See through the eyes of your Brothers and Sisters, and to share their Perceptions.

Questioning is one of the most vital paths to understanding these Stories, which will Teach you of the Sun Dance Way. When you question, the Medicine Wheel is turned for you. These Stories are magical Teachers in this way. They are Flowers of Truth whose petals can be unfolded by the Seeker without end.[4]

The profound understanding here of the work that stories do in revitalizing individual and shared life, the ways they function as mirrors and teachers, their versatility as instruments of healing and growth, gives us some measure of what has been lost in a culture where stories have become, to a large extent, a commodity. Most of our stories are mediated by film. This is not always a loss, though often the two-hour visual format entails unfortunate reduction; some films have become cultural touch-

4. Hyemeyohsts Storm, *Seven Arrows* (New York: Ballantine Books, 1972), p. 10.

stones and continue to provide shared frames of reference or points of contact with a shared past. But films are mostly commercial products, scripted and recorded in such a way that they often subordinate the verbal to the visual. They can be rewound and replayed, but not retold. They may help to draw us into communities as viewers and reviewers, but they engage us in a way that forfeits face-to-face human presence and spontaneous revision.

We're inundated with "stories" in various composite forms. News "stories" increasingly confuse fact and fiction, ranging from the thirty-second sound bite, to the infomercial, to the investigative report, to the docudrama. Film companies routinely buy rights to novels and short stories and put them on the screen. And writers continue to write, though increasingly the pressures of mass culture have a defining influence on the sorts of stories writers produce and publishers accept.

We've all seen "Disneyfied" versions of the invigorating fairy tales which once served the deeper, darker purposes that Bruno Bettelheim outlined in *The Uses of Enchantment.*[5] The sanitized cartoon versions of fairy tales that were once emotionally and psychologically complex enough to take hearers to dark and dangerous places, to leave some problems unresolved, some mysteries unpenetrated, and to acknowledge the realities of

5. Bruno Bettelheim, *The Uses of Enchantment: The Meaning and Importance of Fairy Tales* (East Sussex, U.K.: Gardners Books, 1991).

violence, betrayal, and death in a larger context of hope
— these deprive us of a valuable instrument of reflection. Film versions of novels, more or less true to the
text, have to be judged on their own terms, and films
can do things that novels can't. Nevertheless, the work
that words do to incite the imagination, the way they
resonate and give a reader pause, the way they carry
their particular load of association and allusion is inevitably modified and reduced in the time-bound and visu-
ally predetermined medium of even very verbal films.
The popularity of *The Lord of the Rings,* the Narnia tales,
and other adventure sagas testifies to the appetite and
need for story. But those stories, once co-opted by major media, become fixed as images which, however engaging and skillfully rendered, suppress the intimate,
personal, enlivening process of invention that engages
the mind in life-giving work.

There are movements afoot and individuals deter-
mined to reclaim story as a lively, in-person, relational
event: retreats and writers' conferences where people go
to journal and explore the parameters of their life stories;
faithful librarians who continue Saturday-morning story
time; gatherings of professional and amateur storytellers.
One of the more interesting of these movements is the effort among medical practitioners to retrieve story as a
mode of bio-ethical reasoning.

In her wonderful little book *Medicine as Ministry,* Margaret Mohrmann contrasts the process by which ethics

committees routinely reason about difficult biomedical decisions with a process of reasoning through story: "Patients are people who have names and faces; they have unique lives and unique deaths. To think that appropriate ethical answers can be found by abstracting those real persons out of their grounded, embodied, one-of-a-kind stories is to make a fundamental error in ethical reasoning."[6] Of course the idea of "narrative ethics" applies in other venues, theology being one of them. At the heart of that movement is the recognition that we should not — indeed, we cannot — reason rightly about any human situation without story.

So here's a challenge especially to family and church as sites of storytelling: let's tell stories. Those of us who spend our time in the biblical texts and with the wide waters of literature are stewards of stories in a way that commercial filmmakers can't be. In an "information age," we tend to package and promote exchange of "information" to the exclusion of story, seriously diminishing what we preserve and transmit. What stories offer is, in a sense, the opposite of information, at least in the ways they invite understanding. Stories are pathways. The circles of Dante's hell and purgatory, the long upward winding of Bunyan's pilgrim, Odysseus's journey from Ithaca to Troy and home again, Othello's descent — all show us a

6. Margaret Mohrmann, *Medicine as Ministry* (Cleveland: Pilgrim Press, 1995), p. 6.

way. On that journey the storyteller is a guide who knows what lies around the bend and where the resting places are, and discloses those secrets judiciously, in due time.

Other metaphors for story may be similarly useful. Stories are mirrors; they are windows; they are invitations that beckon us to enter into a new place that becomes curiously like home. Stories are safe spaces that offer refuge from confusion even as they involve us in their own complications, and even though they may threaten our dearly held ideas in ways that are quite real and consequential. In both — in providing refuge and in challenging us — they are instruments of healing.

For all these reasons, the power of story is one we must not abdicate. The church needs to be a place where stories are told, where we are invited back into the stories we live by, and where we come to find ourselves at home again in a dwelling made of words that is reconstructed in every telling. We need good storytellers to keep us alive and imagining. The exercise of the imagination is the training ground of compassion. Stories educate the heart. Stories, like poetry, are related to prayer. They have an incantatory, invocational function. They call forth and focus our dread and desire. They are vehicles of confession, thanksgiving, petition.

Years ago I heard Elie Wiesel speak in a large university auditorium. After an elaborate and appreciative introduction, he walked onto the wide platform with a quiet step, unassumingly, sat down in a chair, and began to tell stories. The old rabbinical response to life questions, "Let me tell you a little story," is one of the treasures of the Judeo-Christian tradition. Stories are the oldest and most valuable equipment we have as a human community and as a people of faith. The power of stories lies not only or even mainly in their explanatory function, or in the ways they mirror a community back to itself, or in the examples they provide, or the analogies. That power lies also in the way stories allow us to focus and give shape to our hopes, and to come to terms with the inexplicable and bewildering freedom we have as creatures made in the image of God.

Who are the great storytellers among us now? Toni Morrison, whose novels retrieve and revise the art of storytelling, offers a model of rich, courageous experimentation as well as an imaginative, resilient fidelity to a complex tradition. Wendell Berry, whose stories reaffirm what we stand to lose in trading the demands of land and community for the dubious conveniences of urban anonymity. Barbara Kingsolver, whose characters struggle with the changing shape of family and survival on the social margins. Rudolfo Anaya, who chronicles bicultural lives lived on very different terms from those of the dominant culture that surrounds them. We have many among us — perhaps too many: when Flannery O'Connor was asked whether university courses in creative writing stifled young writers, she is said to have responded, "They don't stifle enough of them!" But we have much to learn from the best among them. I would hope that as conservators of story we would keep alive in ourselves the love of stories by inventing them, telling them, reading them, embellishing them, and resisting the lure of the video store now and then to content ourselves with words and imaginings. We need to hear one another's voices. We need to hear one another's stories, and we need to tell our own, because, being human, we need to be healed.

Part of that healing is a re-ordering of our expectations. The myths and stories we inherit shape our earliest hopes, sometimes falsely. As stories expand our imagination for alternative ways of living, our disappointments may soften into lessons, and our hopes become deeper and more complex. As Oscar Wilde observed, life imitates art. We derive our basic expectations from the narrative patterns we internalize — the hope of a happy ending, the recognition of the need for sacrifice, a sense of how communities work, an understanding of family. Stories provide the basic plotlines and in the infinite variations on those plots help us to negotiate the open middle ground between predictability and surprise.

Anyone who has read the same story night after night to a child knows how traveling a familiar narrative path through scary places and back to the safety of home and hearth can provide a respite from the confusions of the day. Even tragic tales reassure in the way they remind us of the basic terms of our lives together and how communities survive significant loss. Perhaps their greatest comfort value lies in the way they point beyond themselves to the larger stories of creation and promise and salvation.

Like good sermons, however, stories not only comfort but also "afflict the comfortable." Usually they do this by holding up a mirror in which we recognize our own flaws and faults. For instance, I recently taught Ursula LeGuin's little parable, "The Ones Who Walk Away from Omelas," to a group of nineteen-year-olds, some of whom walked away from class sobered and troubled by the implications of a mythic society whose luxuries and comforts were maintained on the condition that one child be kept in squalid, abusive confinement. The story challenged them to ask, "Can this be an image of the way we live?" — a profoundly disconcerting question that needs to be asked.[7]

Stories like this — mythic, shadowy, parabolic — tell us what we already know but may deny, forget, suppress, distort, or take for granted. Tolkien reminds us that we are on a perilous journey with a promise of good completion. Hawthorne reminds us of corporate sins more destructive than adultery that need to be acknowledged. Austen and Eliot remind us that even the bright and the virtuous like Elizabeth and Dorothea have lessons to learn.

7. Ursula LeGuin, "The Ones Who Walk Away from Omelas," in *The Wind's Twelve Quarters* (New York: Harper & Row, 1975), p. 275.

And so do we. The lessons stories offer involve us, too, in reorganizing our sense of family, our understanding of who wields power, our priorities. The third son claims the inheritance. An unlikely child pulls the sword from the stone. Hansel and Gretel find their way. The pauper turns out to be the prince. The humble are exalted. And so our most basic social expections are reframed. What looks like blessing turns out to be disaster, and what looks like tragedy opens the way to blessing. Conventional notions of happy families, good marriages, and abundance are complicated in ways that surprise us into radical reassessment of our desires.

At their best, if they are doing what they are meant to do, stories help us to cultivate compassion. This, I think, is their primary function. They open our hearts and imaginations. They invite and challenge and tease us into understanding and take us places we might not otherwise consent to go.

Love the Long Sentence

S ome years ago (never mind how long, as Ishmael would say), when I was a graduate student, a friend and I entertained ourselves one evening imagining a course we'd teach titled "Unreadable Novels." These would include, for starters, Joyce's *Finnegan's Wake,* Melville's *The Confidence Man,* Beckett's *The Unnameable,* some imported arcana from postwar French writers like Nathalie Sarraute and Marguerite Duras, a little South American magical realism, and perhaps Pynchon's *Gravity's Rainbow,* which David Quammen referred to as a "great steaming slagheap of a novel."[1] All of them, of course, are quite readable — even exhilarating — if you give them their terms. But they do require that we stretch our conventional notions of what to expect from stories, not to mention our patience. They're good for readers' marathons.

---

1. David Quammen, "The Troubled Gaze of the Octopus," in *Natural Acts: A Sidelong View of Science and Nature* (New York: Avon Books, 1996), p. 18.

I mention them here because many of these novels and some that are better known and not quite so quickly consigned to the "life is too short" category — those of Faulkner and Henry James, for instance — share an underappreciated stylistic feature to which I'd like to draw some appreciative attention: the long sentence. I want to speak for the virtues of the long sentence, to call your attention to its particular pleasures and rewards, and, more pertinently, to suggest that it offers an essential antidote to the sound-bite syndrome I've already identified as a linguistic pathology of our time. I want to commend it to you as a strategy to embrace, albeit selectively, in your own writing and speaking lives, modernism and minimalism notwithstanding. I want to suggest that a good steward of words ought to be able to construct, manage, navigate, and convey the delights of a long sentence, and ought to recognize in a good long sentence an instrument of reflection that can sharpen the life of the mind and foster discernment.

Those are large claims for a writerly habit much discouraged by American editors, though I believe the Germans maintain their tolerance of it rather nicely. No doubt many long sentences need to be cut up into more digestible pieces; some are mere verbal self-indulgence; some are simply "rabbiting on," as my British friend puts it — betokening a rather boorish inability to recognize when the audience has had enough of a good thing; some are the explanatory overkill of condescending pedants.

Love the Long Sentence

But some long sentences take us on journeys worth making from the beginning of an idea through its permuta-
tions and possibilities, gathering modification, nuance,
definition, and direction as it goes. Long sentences ask us
to dwell in a thought rather than come to the point. They
invite us to relax into a slow syntactical tour, like wandering the halls of a museum, rather than hastening onward
to the verb, the object, and out the door.

So let me invite you to tour the back roads of three long
sentences with me and consider what they have to teach
us about hovering, dwelling, musing, reframing, meandering, and enjoying the way words can tease and slow us into
seeing what is only visible to the sustained gaze.

First, let us consider the convoluted, interruptive, labyrin-
thine twelve-line syntactical mazes we find in the prose of
Henry James. These monuments, which arise rather startlingly in the midst of more moderate narrative structures
like high-rises in the suburbs, can be daunting. Admittedly,
they are an acquired taste. The hastening eye, trained to
scan for bullet points, is tempted to search for the period
and move on. And it is not just that they're long, but that
even the shorter sentences around them tend to include at
least one loop through a parenthetical observation, quali-
fying clause, or extended elliptical reference. Moreover, the
wandering orphaned pronoun of uncertain antecedent
appears to be one of James's favorite devices. All these
things make the Jamesian sentence not simply something

to float upon, enjoying the occasional drift and swirl, but something to be navigated with care and close attention to its turns and eddies by the readerly equivalent of a white-water guide.

Let us consider an example from the opening page of *The Ambassadors.* Let us duly note that it *is* the opening page, and therefore the innocent reader's first exposure to this particular plot, character, and setting — perhaps her first exposure to James, if she hasn't been warned not to leap unprepared into these deep waters, but to dabble her feet in *Daisy Miller* first. I will include here three sentences from the opening paragraph. They may offer more than enough difficulties to make my point — which is, to reiterate, that they have good reason to be long, and that their difficulties are gifts.

The same secret principle, however, that had prompted Strether not absolutely to desire Waymarsh's presence at the dock, that had led him thus to postpone for a few hours his enjoyment of it, now operated to make him feel he could still wait without disappointment. They would dine together at the worst, and, with all respect to dear old Waymarsh — if not even, for that matter, to himself — there was little fear that in the sequel they shouldn't see enough of each other. The principle I have just mentioned as operating had been, with the most newly disembarked of the two men, wholly instinctive — the fruit of a sharp sense that, delightful as it would be to find himself looking, after so much separation, into his comrade's face, his business would be a trifle bungled should he simply arrange for this countenance to present itself to the nearing steamer as the first "note" of Europe.[2]

We begin here at the third sentence of the novel. We don't know Strether. We don't know Waymarsh. We don't know at what dock we have arrived, or why, what manner of men we're about to consort with, what "business" is at hand, and why, if the men are friends, one of them should wish the other not to be on hand to greet him after a long separation. Of course, we begin every novel with references to people and events we don't know. But here the references are made in an offhand and elusive manner that seems to assume that we do know, or at least should know, or perhaps infer from the slightest hints, what is at issue that brings Strether to Europe and keeps him from wanting to see Waymarsh. That presumption, along with the interruptive commas and dashes and asides, presents the first little series of what will become familiar frustrations. The bar is set high. But — and here's the heart of the matter — the reader who can clear that bar has already experienced something of the exhilaration of the sprinter who clears the first hurdle. The weak of will, the

2. Henry James, *The Ambassadors* (New York: W. W. Norton, 2d edition, 1994), p. 17.

desultory, and the dallying have been weeded out by the end of the first page. But, to change athletic metaphors, those willing to make the trudge uphill will get the grand view.

The trudge must be taken slowly. Let us remember the three basic questions I ask students to pause over when they venture into a writer's territory for the first time: What does this writer *invite* you to do? What does he or she *require* of you? What does he or she *not let* you do? These questions focus attention upon the "contract" between writer and reader. A story is an invitation, and a challenge, and a choice. If you consent to its terms, you will have your reward, but only if you take it on in the spirit in which it is offered. (N.B.: There are, of course, certain rewards to be gained by the "resisting reader" who refuses the author's terms, challenging and deconstructing the text for his or her own purposes, but even those satisfactions depend upon fully understanding the writer's terms.)

So, to answer my own questions briefly, though many possible answers might apply to *The Ambassadors,* already on the first page James invites you to imagine the story. We not only find ourselves plunged *in medias res,* but into what seem to be the more shadowy recesses of Strether's complex but suppressed emotional life. We are already called upon to begin to know this man from the inside out. We don't know what he looks like, how old he is, where he comes from, or what he does for a living. We don't know, as an Austen character once impatiently put it, "what are his tastes, his habits, his preoccupations." We only have the wispy sense that he has instinctive, intuitive movements of feeling or even whims that he seems to take rather seriously; that those feelings are not vague (rather, they are a "sharp sense"), but they are hard to name. That he is capable of different kinds of enjoyment that, in moments like this one, compete with each other, and that he is capable of treating his pleasures with discernment and discipline, setting one before the other. So we are invited, abruptly and surprisingly, into quite intimate psychic space.

As we enter it, we are required to move slowly. A distinguished professor, lecturing at a major university to a crowd of several hundred students, once observed that one of the hard things about James for most readers is that it takes a James character about four pages to put on his socks. This is true enough to the spirit of James, though I have yet to witness a James character doing something so unseemly in the public space of the written page. Slowing down, for a contemporary reader, is a countercultural act. Nearly everything in the momentum of modern life urges us onward at an accelerating pace. The non-skimmable sentence with an undertow that carries us backward to reconsider almost as strongly as it moves us forward to learn more is a sentence which insists that, to borrow a line from Roethke, we "take our waking slow." In doing so, we are required to consider possibilities, and so actively to hypothesize a story. What might be the relation of the two men? Why might Strether want to put off their meeting? What is he hoping to experience in the intervening hours of solitary arrival? And what is the business he doesn't want to bungle? The very leisure of the sentence gives us space for such pondering and conjecture before allowing us to move on. The disconcerting search for the antecedent (one of James's favorite devices is to bury the antecedent to his frequent pronouns, thus requiring that we retrace our steps to make sure we know what exactly we're still talking about) is even to the purpose in that it makes us consider, much more carefully than we might otherwise be inclined to, the connections between things. And as James himself once put it, "We only understand things in relation." It is in the web of connection that meaning is caught on the wing.

And so the passage prevents us from indulging our vulgar appetites for action, information, and explanation — the fast food of fiction. It prevents us from leaping to conclusions, though it invites us to consider possibilities. It schools us in the very patience it demands.

This discipline, the arduous training in reflection, re-consideration, invention, the capacity I have mentioned for "dwelling in possibility" and exercising "negative ca-pability," is one of James's great gifts to the reader. I would go so far as to call it virtue. To read him well is to practice certain virtues that lay the ground for compassion.

Love the Long Sentence

Faulkner's writing, like James's, requires and rewards patience. In a very different way from James, different in mode and feeling, in his epistemology and even in his eschatology, Faulkner also teaches us to imagine the layers of causality, experience, pain and compensation, unawareness, awareness, suppression, and emotional substitution that lie beneath the surfaces of human behavior and story. His sentences are archaeologies of survival and, to use one of his favorite terms, endurance. Reading them we learn, like apprentices at the master's elbow, to lengthen our gaze and extend our imaginations into the past that presses insistently on the present.

They remind us, as Wendell Berry does, that

> When we reflect that "sentence" means, literally, "a way of thinking" (Latin: *sentential*) and that it comes from the Latin *sentire*, to feel, we realize that the concepts of sentence and sentence structure are not merely grammatical or merely academic — not negligible in any sense. A sentence is both the opportunity and the limit of thought — what we have to think with, and what we have to think in. It is, moreover, a feelable thought, a thought that impresses its sense not just on our understanding, but on our hearing, our sense of rhythm and proportion. It is a pattern of felt sense.[3]

3. Wendell Berry, "Standing by Words," in *Standing by Words* (Washington, D.C.: Shoemaker & Hoard, 2005), p. 53.

This large understanding of what sentences represent and accomplish seems particularly pertinent to Faulkner's sentences, which consistently lead us into psychohistorical depths along steep and precipitous paths, down which the weight of thought carries us with gathering, ominous momentum, often to a final jarring image or a glimpse of apocalypse.

The life of a woman, recapitulated in the next example, is described in other sentences of similar length at intervals throughout the opening chapters of *Absalom, Absalom!* Each reiteration is a new map of her story and a reminder that the many versions of our stories co-exist in memory and imagination, that what we know and remember are fluid, and so every sentence, no matter how capacious and probing, is merely another "way of putting it," another "periphrastic study," as Eliot put it, another reminder of finitude. But listen for the invitation in this one — for the way the sentence asks us and teaches us to imagine this woman's life:

> So for the first sixteen years of her life she lived in that grim tight little house with the father whom she hated without knowing it — that queer silent man whose only companion and friend seems to have been his conscience and the only thing he cared about his reputation for probity among his fellow men — that man who was later to nail himself in his attic and starve to death rather than look upon his native land in the

throes of repelling an invading army — and the aunt who even ten years later was still taking revenge for the fiasco of Ellen's wedding by striking at the town, the human race, through any and all of its creatures — brother nieces nephew-in-law herself and all — with the blind irrational fury of a shedding snake.[4]

These are the terms we are given as necessary to understanding this woman's life: the formative period of sixteen years as a foundation for everything else we are to know about her; the unconscious hatred fostered in an environment of despair and revenge; the formative events, not of her own life but of her father's and her aunt's, that shaped her own before she came to consciousness. The sentence offers a whole way of understanding what "shapes our ends"; it suggests a psychological fatalism that deeply questions free will, the inescapable connections forged before birth to land and ancestors; and a very specific way in which the sins of the fathers may be visited upon the children. That's a lot for one sentence to do.

Two long, interruptive clauses describing the father's character and final act, even as they make clear what the daughter would have found to hate, offer him to our consideration in terms of his own obsessions, limitations, imprisonment in a place and way of life and a rigid religi-

---

4. William Faulkner, *Absalom, Absalom!* (New York: Modern Library, The Corrected Text, 1993), p. 58.

osity and strangling pride that give his suicide tragic dimension, despite the narrowness of his pathetic life. The specific method of that suicide tells its own story within a story, simply and explicitly: he nailed himself in the attic and starved to death. Bruno Bettelheim, reflecting on suicide at a public forum, claimed that if a client told him he intended to commit suicide, he would not ask him why, but how, because that would give him more pertinent information. And if, as he suggested, suicide is always a symbolic act, the simple facts in this sentence provide a wealth of information about the quality of despair the father sustained and transmitted. Similarly, and in a complementary fashion that evokes ancient archetypes from Greek tragedy and myth, the aunt who strikes "with the blind irrational fury of a shedding snake" adds a third term to this story of grim survival and defeat that reinforces the message that despair, hatred, loneliness, and thwarted desire act like poisons in the family and in the psyche, that we are born into a world so fallen that health and love of any degree are miracles.

As in James, we are challenged in sentences like these to allow a larger awareness to dawn on us; not to divert our gaze until we have seen into what we've looked upon, reckoned with its past and its pain, grasped it in a relational context, and perhaps seen the darknesses of our own lives at least fleetingly mirrored back. Such sentences offer both conviction and absolution in giving, so often, a "full look at the worst."

We find long sentences to love not only in prose but also in poetry, where, though they serve similar purposes, they function very differently to stretch us into a kind of "negative capability" that can sustain and even relax into the tensions of cumulative thought without collapsing into closure. Many poets use the tension between short lines and long sentences to sharpen and slow our seeing and sustain our gaze. In poem after poem, Mary Oliver guides us along sentences that hold us suspended and move us on in rhythms like heartbeats, reminding us of the way all living things are both caught in time and held in timeless moments of epiphany when the veil lifts and falls and we go on. Consider her poem "Hawk," what it asks of us, and how it guides us toward whole sight.

Hawk

This morning
   the hawk
      rose up
         out of the meadow's browse

and swung over the lake —
   it settled
      on the small black dome
         of a dead pine,

alert as an admiral,
   its profile

distinguished with sideburns
the color of smoke,

and I said: remember
this is not something
of the red fire, this is
heaven's fistful

of death and destruction,
and the hawk hooked
one exquisite foot
onto a last twig

to look deeper
into the yellow reeds
along the edges of the water
and I said: remember

the tree, the cave,
the white lily of resurrection,
and that's when it simply lifted
its golden feet and floated

into the wind, belly-first,
and then it cruised along the lake —
all the time its eyes fastened
harder than love on some

   unimportant rustling in the
      yellow reeds — and then it
         seemed to crouch high in the air, and then it
            turned into a white blade, which fell.[5]

This long, single-sentence poem could easily be broken into discrete thoughts; many an English teacher would probably suggest putting periods where the dashes stick out at the ends of lines like defensive gestures, as if to say, "Wait! I'm not done yet! Don't stop here!" But that's exactly what they mean. What appear to be points of completion aren't, because to get the whole of what is being offered, we have to travel the whole inclusive trajectory from beginning to end. It takes us from rising to falling, through the stages of encounter and envisioning that move us from imagining the hawk's dignity and beauty to understanding the predatory intent and decisive, destructive power of movements that in themselves look leisurely, unconcerned, and even exquisite. John Fowles's novel *Daniel Martin* begins with this curious sentence: "Whole sight; or all the rest is desolation."[6] Oliver's poems encourage us toward whole sight in their visual scope, the way they take fully into account both perceiving subject and perceived object as aspects of a single event contained in an implied

5. Mary Oliver, "Hawk," in *New and Selected Poems* (Boston: Beacon Press, 1992), p. 34.

6. John Fowles, *Daniel Martin* (Boston: Back Bay Books, reprint edition, 1987), p. 1.

larger awareness, and simply in their sustained sentences. The "and . . . and . . . and . . ." narrative is not simply cumulative, but fugue-like in its unfolding what is being enacted and witnessed, line by complicating line. The import of what the speaker sees does not simply accumulate but gets denser with felt meaning. Surprising words and phrases stop us: "browse," "sideburns," "fistful," "exquisite," "harder than love," "white blade." Each unusual choice reframes and enables us to re-imagine what we might otherwise pass over.

All lyric poems, especially unrhymed, free-verse poetry like this, use the tension between line and sentence as a way of delivering meaning on at least two distinct levels. The end of each short line opens out into white space and silence that momentarily cues us to stop and take in the image or phrase without further syntactical context before going on. These increments are not ideas, or even thoughts, but images, impressions, fleeting strands of feeling that precede statement. They call themselves to our intuitive awareness before we are allowed to see them as part of a rational structure.

And this is, of course, how we take things in — in bits and fragments, sense impressions surfacing, suggesting, reminding, pointing toward something that hasn't come clear yet, that we may anticipate but that may yet surprise us. Oliver's poems enact epiphany as a way in which what is evident and manifest may suddenly become what Eliot called "a shocking revaluation." Sudden light shines through the hawk, and we see that he is both predator and messenger. If we stay the course and complete the sentence, we will receive the vision, but the sentence is long, and only those who learn to love the long sentence, only the slow, win the gift.

Practice Poetry

Anyone who has taken walks with small children knows that "getting there" is not the point. They stop and squat down. They smell plants. They laugh at dog poop. They pick up bugs. They drop the pebble they've been carrying, start to look for it, and find a feather instead. The feather turns out to be so satisfactory that they forget about the pebble. And where you end up, which may or may not be where you thought you were going, turns out to be the place you were going all the time.

Goal-oriented adults have to work hard to retrieve the habits of mind and heart I'm describing — the unself-conscious playfulness that will stop over anything and take an interest, the openness to noticing the random and irrelevant — indeed, to retrieve the basic attitude that nothing is random or irrelevant. This is the work that poetry requires and enables.

It is my experience that poems begin in that state of mind. I know that some poets are methodical and consistent in the practice of their craft, and I admire them. But many poems come in the midst of doing something else — usually something quite unpoetic: making dinner, looking for a parking place or keys or glasses. They come as gifts — little phrases or images that flutter into awareness and distract it from its linear progress toward some more pedestrian objective.

There is a gift character to all poems; theorize as we might, experience insists that they "come from someplace," beyond the conscious and controlling mind, and that those who write them are recipients and owe a debt of gratitude for the satisfying phrase or image or verb. The intuitive moment of noticing something old as though it were new is inherently childlike: the "Hey, look!" moment. The occurring seems relational. The response is "Hey! Thank you! Yes! I'll write that down." In that writing down, the work and craft begin, and the deliberate rendering of line and meter. It is a collaboration.

What the discipline of poetry requires most of all is caring about words and caring for words. I do not believe we steward language well without some regular practice of *poesis* — reading poetry, learning some by heart, and writing — if not verse as such, at least sentences crafted with close attention to cadence and music and the poetic devices that offer nonrational, evocative, intuitive, associative modes of understanding. To return to the ecological metaphor I suggested in the opening chapter — that stewardship of the word is akin to stewardship of other resources — it might be useful to recognize how poets, like ecologists, are finding new ways to utter the call to remembrance that dates back to the Psalms and beyond: Remember that you are dust, a mortal creature sharing the earth with others. Remember the voice that speaks in the wind. Remember the refiner's fire. Remember, as Lao Tse taught, that the way of the wise one is the way of water.[1] As we become more and more detached from whole process, from the cycle of seasons, planting and harvest, building and making by hand, we need these reminders more urgently: that we are made from this earth; that, as Donne put it, "No man is an island," and as Whitman put it, "Every atom belonging to me as good belongs to you," and as Eliot put it, "The river is within us; the sea is all around us."

In his humane and useful reflections on poetry, *How Does a Poem Mean?* John Ciardi recalls a story that defines the essential difference between the poetic habit of mind and the conventional:

> W. H. Auden was once asked what advice he would give a young man who wished to become a poet. Auden replied that he would ask the young man why he wanted

1. Lao Tse, *Tao Te Ching,* trans. Jonathan Star (Los Angeles: Jeremy Tarcher, 2001), p. 259.

to write poetry. If the answer was "because I have something important to say," Auden would conclude that there was no hope for that young man as a poet. If on the other hand the answer was something like "because I like to hang around words and overhear them talking to one another," then that young man was at least interested in a fundamental part of the poetic process and there was hope for him.[2]

One of the hardest quantum leaps in studying literature as a discipline is learning to look *at* words rather than *through* them — to "hang around" them and listen rather than assuming command, and to trust that what will come of this apparently unproductive practice, "leaning and loafing," as Whitman put it, will be immensely worthwhile. We can't always predict what words will do under these circumstances, allowed a little of their own inertial energy; as in so many other situations, relinquishing our habits of control may bring unanticipated pleasures.

That relinquishment may, on the other hand, bring unanticipated frustration. Every writer who has struggled to make a stanza or paragraph presentable has known the truth of Eliot's lament: "Words strain,/Crack and sometimes break, under the burden,/Under the tension, slip, slide, perish,/Decay with imprecision, will not

2. John Ciardi and Miller Williams, *How Does a Poem Mean?* (Boston: Houghton Mifflin, 1960), p. 667.

stay in place,/Will not stay still."[3] As that happens, as commercial culture and media magnates dumb down the language and press it into degrading servitude to profit and propaganda, the business of using language well becomes a reclamation project of proportions similar to those undertaken in seventeenth-century Holland when the citizens decided to retrieve almost a third of their slowly submerging land from the sea. Everyone who writes with care, who treats words with respect and allows even the humblest its historical and grammatical dignity, participates in the exhilarating work of reclamation. Each essay or poem is its own "raid on the inarticulate," and every written work that forestalls the slow death of speech is a response to Wendell Berry's challenge to "practice resurrection."[4] When we slow down in the way that careful writing requires, enough to taste and savor words, we begin to rediscover how delectable and succulent are the fruits that hang on the tree of language, closely engrafted as it is to the tree of life.

Some years ago a hapless economics major condemned by general education requirements to take my poetry course wandered into my office in a state of slight

3. T. S. Eliot, *Burnt Norton,* in *The Complete Poems and Plays of T. S. Eliot* (New York: Harcourt, Brace & World, 1971), p. 121.

4. T. S. Eliot, *East Coker,* in *The Complete Poems and Plays of T. S. Eliot,* p. 128; Wendell Berry, "The Mad Farmer: Liberation Front," in *Collected Poems of Wendell Berry, 1957-1982* (San Francisco: North Point Press, 1987), p. 151.

frustration with our leisurely, close readings of Hopkins, Eliot, Plath, et al. She asked, "Why do people do this?" Here's the subtext to that question as I understood it: Why would people take time to linger over poetry, sniff at words, pick them up and look under them, and ponder the logic of line breaks when there are important things to do in the world? There's the national debt to worry about (and of course this objection might be much more forcefully made at present), space shuttles to construct and launch, the terms of trade and commerce to renegotiate yet again. So why spend this kind of time on a poem?

It is a reasonable question, given the state of poetry in contemporary American culture. Although a great deal of poetry is still being written, published, read in public, and even memorized, it plays a role more marginal than in any other culture or generation I know of in public, political, and ecclesial discourse. We give a nod to the tradition of the poet laureate by having one who gets a year to go on the circuit and remind the American public that poems matter. But by and large, the writing and reading of poetry takes place either in classrooms by requirement, or in venues where the poetically inclined gather over coffee or in the modest spaces of bookstores to share the word wealth so many ignore. So my student's question deserved some thought, and I gave it some. The world is in more of a mess than it was when the question was posed, the terms of vigilant citizenship in nation, world, and kingdom more vexed, and all our daily tasks

149

multiplied and complicated by convenience technologies, so the justification for what might seem an effete occupation of the academic elite or those who like nightlife in cafes might seem even less self-explanatory than it might once have been.

Indeed, there are good reasons not to engage in the practice of poetry. Poetry is not profitable. There's a great deal of bad poetry out there that really is a waste of time. Poetry takes quality time that for most of us is a limited commodity. And many of us, alas, suffered the malpractice of some English teacher who made the work of poesis into drudgery. We need to find those teachers and rehabilitate them.

The reasons to read poetry take longer to articulate. The most persuasive, if one is willing to entertain it, is that reading and writing poetry are survival skills. If we learn the skills involved in reading closely, attentively, imaginatively, if we understand the demands of a poem and respond to them, we are better equipped to negotiate flexibly, distinguish what is authentic from what is false, and make discerning decisions. But poetry's demands are complex. Poems demand that we slow down, notice patterns, reckon with ambiguities, consider subtle distinctions between one term or image and its alternative, and recognize the relationship between techniques and purposes. But if we take this work on, if we practice finding paths through poems, staying with them as we tease out their possibilities, follow where they point us by allusion and suggestion, and unpack their metaphors, they can equip us to walk into any situation, look around, assess, analyze, and act. They teach us to listen more attentively to language and to reckon more astutely with the arts of persuasion. More than that, they restore to us what I believe the noise and haste of commercial culture dull and destroy: being attuned to subtleties of sense and feeling, being awake to the possibilities of "an ordinary moment on an ordinary day." They train and exercise the imagination.

Trained imaginations are what we need most at a time like this. That is what will enable us to reach across cultures and understand each other, to think of new models and modes of organization that might work better, and to wage peace, because the love of beauty is deeply related to the love of peace. Beauty and peace are things to be learned and protected, because we see all too much evidence around us that they can be lost. Think of the wide-angle vision provided not only in the Psalms, with their great range of feeling and experience, but also in modern poems like Yeats's "The Second Coming" or Eliot's *Four Quartets,* both of which call us to a large view of what is happening to us all and to take it personally. They invite us to find the still point in the midst of the "turning world" and look from there with horror and pity at what remains to be healed.

The practice of *lectio divina,* which I mentioned earlier as a foundation for enriching our lives as readers, can extend widely to include all poetry worth reading. Reading to be addressed, finding the word or phrase that speaks to us, pausing there, receiving it as invitation, resting in it as a word for the moment, we receive words we need from poetry as well as from Scripture. To read well is to let the Spirit work, as it does when lines and phrases we know resurface again and again to remind us of something true.

As a stay against crass, prosaic, and unimaginative language, good poetry offers us all this. We need it, not in the same way we need sacred Scripture, but for what it offers us that we can take back to our reading of those foundational texts and our understanding of the natural world and of human affairs that cannot be developed any other way. As irreducibly as mathematics, we need it as a tool for understanding our world. We have a responsibility to read it well, to let it teach us love of words and to receive it as the gift that it is for the benefit of the whole body.

Distilling all these thoughts to answer my student's question, I brought it down to two points: "One, poetry makes me happy, and two, I can't think of many things that are more useful than this." At this she raised a skeptical eyebrow, so I elaborated: "Language is the basic tool for preserving civilization. It seems useful to understand as much as we can about how it works since it's arguably one of the most potent forms of power that society has produced — that and the atom-splitter."

A colleague of mine in the biology department had a student who complained in a similar vein that studying the microbes on an eyelash somehow ruined the mystery of visible beauty by making us aware of organic life crawling all over everything we look at. When he finished laughing, he replied that every time you uncover a mystery, you find a greater one — and that was the joy of biology. Everyone who has ever walked a class through a poem has encountered the same sort of resistance: "Why are we going to ruin this lovely poem by dissecting it?" This is where I replace their metaphorical corpse with a live body and make my "analysis is an act of love" speech. It's not just a rhetorical trick; analysis *is* an act of love. Reading slowly, carefully, looking for pattern, considering word choice, the logic of line breaks, figures of speech, pondering the fitness of images — these require a quality of attention that is comparable to the kind of attention a lover pays the beloved — noticing and noticing. A bit of wisdom from musician Roberto Gerhard that hung on the wall of my library carrel to spur me through my dissertation year gets quoted to all my poetry students: "Attention — deep, sustained, undeviating — is in itself an experience of a very high order."

Among the most satisfying moments in teaching a poetry class are those when a student not already predisposed to enjoy poetry learns how to enter a poem and walk around inside it. These moments of insight usually come upon him or her quite suddenly, like the moment the child on her first bike gets her balance. It was not for mere novelty that Howard Nemerov wrote a landmark essay on the similarity between poems and jokes.[5] And, as Barry Sanders points out, Chaucer preceded him "in stroke of brilliance" by noticing that "the physicality of the practical joke could be converted into a verbal punch line" and delivering those lines in the context of poems.[6] The moment of "getting it" is one of startling double vision — a sudden shift of frame that sets an ordinary thing ablaze with new significance and frequently elicits laughter of recognition. Moments of truth, when they burst upon us, seem to be validated by laughter.

One of the most memorable of these moments of revelation was that of my student Rebecca. She was a returning student, a single mother struggling to finish college on a part-time salary. She sat in the front row. She came to office hours regularly once a week, *Norton Anthology* in hand, usually to announce that she hadn't "gotten it" yet. "I look at the poem," she would tell me, "and sometimes I feel what a powerful poem it is, but I can't find my way into it. I don't know what to do when it's sitting there in front of me. I know you've shown us

5. Howard Nemerov, "Bottom's Dream: The Likeness of Poems and Jokes," in *Reflections on Poetry and Poetics* (New Brunswick, N.J.: Rutgers University Press, 1972).

6. Barry Sanders, *A Is for Ox* (New York: Pantheon Books, 1994), p. 106.

how, but I don't seem to know how to ask the right questions when I'm alone."

We walked through a lot of poems together. Ask *how,* not *what,* I reminded her, to forestall the reductive moralizing that so often passes for analysis. Don't ask the big questions — ask the small questions. They're the big questions in disguise. Why did he pick this word? Why did she choose to end the line here? What happens when the regular rhythm is broken in the third line? What shifts the tone in the final couplet? Stop over anything that makes you pause. Let yourself stop and circle back and take a word or an image in your hand and turn it over and consider how it's behaving. If you march through the poem, left to right, top to bottom, you'll be at the end of the page very quickly, having navigated the road but missed the landscape. Poems trick you that way. You have to learn to read all over again, or you'll miss them altogether; they'll be over in sixty seconds, and you'll wonder where you've been.

Rebecca knew all this. Her natural advantage was a high susceptibility to the powers of language and rhythm. She herself had a quality of unself-conscious grace that made the most prosaic sentence sound like song. Working with her, I felt the ambivalence that must strike anyone who trains a natural talent — a certain reluctance to domesticate the wild rightness of instinct. Her expressive gift was exceeded by only two things: humility and desire. More than anything, she wanted to learn that year to master poetry, read it with authority, possess it, and speak it with a right of ownership that can be gained only by putting in time and submitting to the slow acculturation that every good poem, being its own country, demands.

The poems we read that semester spanned a wide spectrum of appeal. Often, picking poems for class, I would think especially of Rebecca, wondering which one would offer her a breakthrough into a new level of reading. The moment came, but not when I expected it. It was not the writers of the Harlem Renaissance, where the content might have touched a chord of common culture. It was not Bishop or Plath or Rich, or any of the women in whom I thought she might recognize the "dream of a common language." Rebecca found her key to poetry in Robert Frost — that crusty old New Englander with his stubborn regionalism, whose words so often led downward into darkness rather than rising toward song.

One Thursday afternoon she appeared at the threshold of my office, clutching her anthology to her bosom with unusual fervor. She came in, sat on the edge of her chair, and held the aging paperback as if it were alive. She announced, "I know how to do this now." She opened the book to a place in the middle where the page was folded down and wrinkled from thumbing. "I want to show you."

She read the title, "After Apple-Picking," then paused, like the preacher about to begin the gospel. Line by line she went through the poem, lifting each line to the light

to show me how it worked, reading it again to allow it all
its resonance, then reaching backward to weave internal
connections.

> I cannot rub the strangeness from my sight
> I got from looking through a pane of glass
> I skimmed this morning from the drinking
>   trough . . .[7]

"I've never seen a sheet of ice on water like that," she said,
"but I can see how it would make the things on the other
side distorted and strange." She squinted slightly as she
spoke, as if peering through the ice pane. She'd never
seen a drinking trough, either. She'd never left her little
urban plot of California. Never set foot in New England,
perhaps never seen apples ripe for picking. The web of
references was as foreign as it was meant to be familiar.
Frost with his homely speech and earthy imagery gave
her the shock of recognition that art so often provides in
merging the familiar and the strange. "I had to look up
russet," she said. "I like that word."

Her rich voice gave full resonance to the "rumbling
sound/Of load on load of apples coming in." And there
was audible tragedy in the admission, "For I have had
too much/Of apple-picking: I am overtired/Of the great

7. Robert Frost, "After Apple-Picking," in *The Poetry of Robert
Frost* (New York: Holt, Rinehart & Winston, 1969).

harvest I myself desired." Then she came to my own favorite line:

> There were ten thousand thousand fruit to touch,
> Cherish in hand, lift down, and not let fall.

"That second 'thousand,'" she said, "makes all the difference." It does. And hear the quality of attentiveness that each of the verbs describes: "touch," "cherish," "lift down," "not let fall." Every moment in this harvesting is a little recognition of preciousness, an effort to save each apple from going "surely to the cider-apple heap/As of no worth."[8]

I can't read "After Apple-Picking" now without thinking of Rebecca. She claimed an inheritance from Frost, as all of us who read take possession of our heritage from forebears who called us by names we didn't know until we heard them whispered in the words of a poem or story.

When I teach poetry, especially poems I love, I go to great lengths to warn against the falsehoods of sentimentality. Legitimate emotion takes its form from intimate, intelligent, intentional engagement. Part of the training is to allow oneself to be touched deeply but not too easily, to learn to be both demanding and yielding, like a dancer with a skilled partner both equally committed to dancing well. It is important to ask much of poems, believing that, as in the

8. Frost, "After Apple-Picking."

larger economy of things, you receive only in the measure that you ask, and what you ask of things will be given.

So poems, besides being something like jokes, are reminders of basic spiritual truths, reminders of the value and validity of intuitive skills. They invite the high play mentioned earlier — the childlike, delighted messing around with words and meanings, with the knowledge that sooner or later a moment of surprise will happen.

Billy Collins's wonderful poem on teaching poetry, as well as anything I know, gets at the difference between the life-giving practice of poetry and the abusive pedantry to which it is often subjected. Though he asks students to take a poem and "hold it up to the light/like a color slide," or "press an ear against its hive," or "water-ski" across its surface, they seem often to "begin beating it with a hose/To find out what it really means."[9] I'd like to suggest that those of us whose concern is to care for words need to preserve poetry from that sad fate. Whether our primary work with words is writing sermons, interpreting legal briefs, or trying to get a straight story from the evening news, poetry can teach us specific skills that we need now more than ever to cultivate if we are to retain a capacity for subtlety. We need skills for complex problem-solving, cross-cultural sensitivity,

9. Billy Collins, "Introduction to Poetry," in *Poetry 180: An Anthology of Contemporary Poems,* ed. Billy Collins (New York: Random House, 2003).

awareness of process and of power relations, ways to re-imagine human community. We need the kind of precision we find in good poems to counteract the "general mess of imprecision" (Eliot again) — as sharp and demanding as the close focus on structures and relations you learn in chemistry or math. It is the precision that Pound insisted on when he defined the image as "that which presents an intellectual and emotional complex in an instant of time . . . which gives that sense of sudden liberation; that sense of freedom from time limits and space limits; that sense of sudden growth, which we experience in the presence of the greatest works of art."[10]

Consider, for instance, how exact, efficient, shocking, and densely allusive is Plath's memorable description of "skin like a Nazi lampshade." Or how accurately Hopkins gets at a particular quality of need in the final line of a prayer in time of spiritual frustration: "Mine, O thou Lord of life, send my roots rain." Or how Dickinson's haunting description of the way "a certain Slant of light/Winter afternoons/ . . . oppresses, like the Heft/of Cathedral Tunes" confuses the senses just enough to evoke quick reassessments of felt experience and fleeting, haunting associations that become available for reflection. When you allow yourself to be stopped suddenly and find your memories realigned by a surprising verb, you participate

10. Ezra Pound, "Vorticism," in *Gaudier-Brzeska: A Memoir* (New York: New Directions, 1970), p. 92.

in the practice of poetry by making yourself vulnerable to the action of the poem. You come into the curious intimacy shared by those who seek the healing word and search through the heap of broken images for a Rosetta stone that will speak across our differences, past our brokenness to a place of knowing.

Consider the way we are invited to attend more closely to the paradox of letting go and hanging on that comes with old age in Shakespeare's Sonnet 73:

> That time of year thou mayest in me behold
> When yellow leaves, or none, or few, do hang
> Upon those boughs which shake against the cold,
> Bare ruin'd choirs, where late the sweet birds sang.[11]

In this passage Shakespeare has given us a feel for old age — as in others he has given us a feel for love or jealousy or loss — in metaphors simple and true enough to have withstood erosion into cliché, and to have served many as a mirror and a lamp on the last leg of their journeys.

Like metaphor, paradox as a habit of mind preserves us from simplistic linearity and literalism and keeps us attentive to the complex ways in which, so often, the opposite is also true. This habit of mind is deeply biblical;

11. William Shakespeare, "Sonnet 73," in *William Shakespeare: The Sonnets,* ed. Douglas Bush and Alfred Harbage (New York: Penguin Books, reprint, 1977), p. 93.

indeed, to listen for the uses of paradox in Jesus' recorded teachings is to recognize how it always points us to a higher plane of understanding. To grasp paradox is a prerequisite not only for fathoming spiritual truths (and every spiritual tradition resorts to paradox to get at what is true as if there is no more direct route to truth), but also for thinking complexly and compassionately about this-worldly issues that affect us daily: how the rich may be poor; how power is a form of vulnerability; how saying no may be a way of saying yes.

Poetic usage lies not only in paradox and play, but in the small acts of renewal that we see in inventive word choice. It may be that Robert Herrick's most valuable gift to English poetry lies in a single word — the "liquefaction" of Julia's clothes. And it may be that Mary Oliver, who continues her work among us even as we speak, is called specifically to remind us how to see beyond the thousand sentimentalities that have fogged our understanding of natural processes and to restore vigor and newness to the way we see sunrises and sunsets ("igniting the fields"), and even vultures who "minister to the grassy miles."[12]

It is not only at the level of word choice and image, however, that poems can teach us to see differently.

12. Mary Oliver, "Morning at Great Pond," in *American Primitive* (Boston: Little, Brown, 1978), and "Vultures," in *New and Selected Poems* (Boston: Beacon Press, 1992).

Poems can educate us about complex systems because that's what they are: they engage our various faculties and modes of understanding simultaneously. They teach us to reframe, to engage ambiguity, to deepen and lengthen our capacity for attention. A good poem will model and require a quality of attention that can transform our vision and make it not only more precise but also more capable of gratitude and awe. Consider, for instance, these lines from Theodore Olson about the fall of a hawk and how that event comes to seem shocking, miraculous, and full of grace:

> This was the perilous, lovely way the hawk fell
> Down the long hill of the wind, the anarch air
> Shaped by his going: air become visible, bent
> To a blade of beauty, cruel and taut and bare,
> A bow of ecstasy, singing and insolent.[13]

Every word of description adds a dimension to our sense of what we are witnessing in this breathtaking fall of a powerful bird of prey. To see this way fosters not only gratitude but compassion for the creatures we behold. The sustained gaze required to find the adequate word engages us in contemplation and reminds us of the worthiness of what is given to us to witness.

13. Theodore Olson, "Hawk's Way," in *Hawk's Way* (The League to Support Poetry, 1941).

Richard Wilbur's poem "The Eye" concludes with a prayer for the kind of seeing for which poetry trains us:

Charge me to see
In all bodies the beat of spirit,
Not merely in the *tout en l'air*
Or double pike with layout

But in the strong,
Shouldering gait of the legless man,
The calm walk of the blind young woman
Whose cane touches the curbstone.
. . . .
Let me be touched
By the alien hands of love forever,
That this eye not be folly's loophole
But giver of due regard.[14]

It takes time and intention and a slow, sustained gaze to be a "giver of due regard." In a course I taught on the literature of the natural world, I used to give students the assignment to go outside, sit for half an hour before a natural object — a rock, a patch of grass, a bush, a tree — and describe it. No digression from simple description. Just see what's there and give it words — and they weren't

14. Richard Wilbur, "The Eye," in *Richard Wilbur: New and Collected Poems* (New York: Harcourt Brace Jovanovich, 1988), p. 57.

to stop writing for the full half-hour. They generally left the classroom doubtful, convinced that after three minutes the job would be done, and found that a half hour was easily, if arduously, fillable with more to see and words to see it with than they anticipated. The words came as they stayed their gaze.

Time spent on seeing like this is never lost. Nor is time spent internalizing that seeing in the practice of memorization. Lines known by heart come when you need them. There are lines that make us plunge further into our griefs and rise further into our pleasures, that help us to know our own lives better, to take fuller possession of our experience. So poetry works to help us become persons "upon whom nothing is lost." I know a woman who comes very near to that ideal who keeps a notebook of poems to memorize. "I don't quite have this one yet," she'll say, flipping the book open to her latest entry. "I get a few words at a time. A few words each day are nourishment enough." Word by word, the poems we memorize restore to us something that slips away in the polluted streams of ordinary language and lead us to places of clarity and quietness.

Even secular poetry is, in its way, a kind of prayer — speech of the spirit that reaches beyond the flatlands of prose and rises into the high country of desire and imagination or into places of feeling where only metaphor can reach. The metaphorical habit of mind, one of the principal fruits of practicing poetry, allows us to penetrate walls of abstraction and arrive at truths accessible only by its means. Metaphor teaches us radical connectedness: that in this world of the five senses, all things bear meaning in relation to one another.

Think, for instance, how richly and consistently biblical metaphors reaffirm our relationship to the natural world and in doing so teach us about our relationship to God. Images of water, rock, light, fire, and wind enable us to recognize the movement of the Spirit in all of creation. Images of food — bread and wine, milk and honey, meat and drink — offer particular insight into the radical intimacy of a God who enters into and participates in the most physical facts of life in the body. Animal images — the dove, the raven, the lion, the great fish — invite us to reflect on our likeness to other orders of being. And images drawn from human occupation — builder and shepherd, bridegroom and bride, warrior and king, father, mother, and child — not only mirror the rich diversity of relationship necessary to human community, but also show how all of those are gathered into relationship with a God who is more variously and persistently present than we think.

Each of these images is "a way of putting it." To borrow a line from one of Mark Van Doren's sonnets about love, "There is no single way it can be told."[15] To practice poetry is to stay accountable to the largeness and mystery of truth

---

15. Mark Van Doren, "Sonnet XXV," in *Collected Poems, 1922-1938* (New York: Henry Holt & Co., 1939), p. 228.

by playing at its edges, peering into it, and finding "what will suffice." Wallace Stevens characterizes the work of the poet in that way in "Of Modern Poetry." The poem inventories what poetry must do to be sufficient to its task:

> It has to be living, to learn the speech of the place.
> It has to face the men of the time and to meet
> The women of the time. It has to think about war
> And it has to find what will suffice.
>
> . . . .
>   It must
> Be the finding of a satisfaction . . .[16]

I'd like to linger momentarily on that last word. It is a modest word but, in its understated way, recalls the promise that our deepest hunger will be "satisfied." It has a surprising sufficiency when we see it in the context of Eliot's Magi recalling their discovery of the Christ child: "It was, you may say, satisfactory." To be satisfied, to find what is sufficient, is specifically not to be indulged or flooded with excess, but to find that a need may be so precisely met that it gives way to contentment. I think of a woman I particularly admire for her serenity who, when I expressed that admiration, simply said, "I have tried to

16. Wallace Stevens, "Of Modern Poetry," in *The Palm at the End of the Mind: Selected Poems and a Play,* ed. Holly Stevens (New York: Vintage, 1971), p. 239.

take to heart the idea of 'striving in all things to be content.'" She seemed like a person satisfied, and her happiness a witness against the frenetic substitutes for happiness whose idiom is hyperbole.

So poetry seeks words "sufficient" to our needs. It also seeks what is sufficient to our dreams and visions — dimensions of knowledge inaccessible to ordinary speech. In that work, poetry serves the hard work of prophecy. We need only look at the book of Revelation to recognize how finally poetic language is the only way to get at what is inaccessible to experience as we know it on this limited plane. Or at Yeats's "Second Coming" — a poem whose prophetic accuracy has continued to surprise as history has unfolded since 1913:

> Turning and turning in the widening gyre
> The falcon cannot hear the falconer;
> Things fall apart; the centre cannot hold;
> Mere anarchy is loosed upon the world,
> The blood-dimmed tide is loosed, and everywhere
> The ceremony of innocence is drowned;
> The best lack all conviction, while the worst
> Are full of passionate intensity.

The ominous images that follow of a sphinx with "a gaze blank and pitiless as the sun," and reeling "shadows of the indignant desert birds," and finally the thought of a "rough beast, its hour come round at last," that "slouches towards Bethlehem to be born"[17] serve to articulate the deep, apocalyptic fears that accompany the precarious rise and inevitable fall of empires, the loss of civility and restraint, the Orwellian or Huxleyan visions of a "brave new world" governed by fear and the blank, impervious face of unchecked power. The language of prophecy is poetry. In its prophetic capacity, poetry can take us to the darkest places. We need to go there — beyond the barricades of denial and false comfort, into the valley of the shadow — to find the only hope worth having.

What brings us to that hope is love. Love is the energy that fuels the whole enterprise of wrestling with words and meanings — the longing to see the source of being and meaning "face to face." Poetry brings us closer to that unsettling and reassuring encounter. Eugene Peterson claims that "to eyes that can see, every bush is a burning bush." Poems, when they are doing what they do best, offer us a glimpse of that fire.

17. W. B. Yeats, "The Second Coming," in *Collected Poems of W. B. Yeats,* 2d rev. ed. (New York: Scribner's, 1996), p. 187.

Attend to Translation

Years ago I translated a couple of books from French to English, and a few articles and poems from German to English. These were modest endeavors, undertaken in my callow youth, but some of the important learning moments in my life of attending to language. What I learned as a translator was this.

Language is culture. Every language has a host of cultural assumptions imbedded in its structure, syntax, and vocabulary: about the relationship of the physical to the spiritual world, about the nature of time, about causality, about courtesy, about basic political and social order. Translation involves one in matters much more complex than finding word equivalencies. There are no exact equivalents.

To translate is to originate. Though his or her accountabilities are different from those of a poet writing in a native language, the translator no less than the original poet imagines and invents the text. Its musicality, its resonance, its allusiveness, its readability, its affective appeal — all rely on the craft of the translator as much as that of the author.

A translator has to deal with competing responsibilities — to the author, to the audience, to the traditions from which the text is being exported and into which the text is being imported, and, in many cases, to previous translators of the same work — and with competing values when accessibility competes with fidelity to the original culture; when the aesthetic value of the idiomatic competes with the obligation to be accurate.

This is not news to the many in universities and seminaries who have been involved in translation at a much more complex and consequential level as biblical translators. The boldness and humility called for in that work are edifying to contemplate. The history of the Bible in English is a history of controversy, theological warfare, wrestling with responsibility and freedom, with the nature of the Word, and with the power of the word. At the latest count, the Old and the New Testaments have, either entirely or in substantial selections, been translated into 2,010 different languages. And the vast weight of commentary and interpretation bears, literally, on every word, sentence, verse, chapter, and book of both Testaments. In certain traditions in Judaism, it bears on every individual letter. Especially coming from Hebrew and Greek into English, the variables are so multiple as to defy any simplistic ideas of how God speaks in sacred texts. It must feel like tampering. It is tampering.

And it is necessary work, not only for those specially called to translate Scripture or other significant texts, but for any of us who hope to speak a word of truth or healing that challenges the dominant discourse of the culture. The business of translation — to make what is inaccessible available, to alter the terms of argument for the sake of being understood, to step inside others' conceptual frameworks and systems of reference and meet them there — belongs to all of us. Those who care for the word carry the word into new contexts and adapt it to new situations.

As I mentioned in the opening chapter, 80 percent of the information stored in the world's computers is in English. English has achieved a dominant place in global discourses that is unprecedented, even at the height of the British Empire. And Americans, insulated on two sides by oceans and on a third perhaps by a historical attitude of entitlement, are largely monolingual. This makes our use of language outside our own local and national contexts a serious diplomatic issue.

In her book *The Need for Words,* Patsy Rodenburg observes, "The attachments each of us has as a nation to words and their rhythms can turn speaking into a territorial issue with very restricted boundaries." And, discussing the highly charged regional differences among speakers of the same language in South Africa, Northern Ireland, Belgium, Canada, and the "free" states of the former Soviet Union, she warns, "Both languages and dialects drive us apart. . . . Make no mistake about it: language, choice of words, and particularly accent can trace contentious lines of battle. Hate and nationalism need words just as much as conciliation and diplomacy do."[1] At international conferences, arrangements for devices and personnel can be an intricately costly business, ridden with diplomatic potholes because to speak one of the dominant languages is privilege, but to accommodate the presence of those whose languages are spoken only by small populations is costly. Henry James once spoke of the predicament of those who speak "small" or minor languages as "a complex fate" — a phrase that in Jamesian dialect suggests something sorrowful indeed. At least it is important to recognize how the burden of accommodation rests somewhat unfairly on them.

Rodenburg gives a more homely example of the kinds of misunderstanding that need to be addressed intentionally and charitably in recalling her own childhood in England, being visited by Dutch relatives: "I would listen with keen curiosity as misunderstandings were aggravated simply by opposing attitudes to words. The Dutch aunts and uncles never seemed to know 'how to behave' according to us. The English side of the family was shocked, for instance, by the blunt and 'rude' replies of

1. Patsy Rodenburg, *The Need for Words* (New York: Theatre Art Books, 1993), pp. 82-84.

the Dutch. . . . The Dutch just were not interested in po-
liteness for its own sake."[2] Conversely, she comments also
on the bemusement of non-English acquaintances at the
British habit of indirection, words used as "delaying tac-
tics," and charm and irony used to deflect sometimes
needed confrontation.

The layers of language difference that separate us extend from whole categories of experience indigenous to
one language culture and not another, to nuances that
distinguish a local dialect from that spoken in the next
valley. In light of those differences and the delicate business of establishing common investment in peace and
community across the globe, it behooves those of us who
care about words to care not only for our native language
but also for what I will call the "biodiversity" of the earth's
languages.

I asked a linguist friend who has worked on helping to
preserve the language of a nearly extinct tribal people in
northern California how she would answer the question
she must encounter: Why should we care if an isolated and
little-spoken tongue dies off? In response, she also used the
metaphor of biodiversity, and she went on to explain that
every language offers unique ways of understanding the
world that are lost to us all when it goes. Even if only a few
vestigial contacts remain between a dying language and
the larger language cultures around it, the possibility of

2. Rodenburg, *The Need for Words,* p. 83.

cross-pollinization remains, and the vision that may be a corrective to what is seen through and framed by another linguistic lens.

Most of us aren't likely to learn Inuit or Navajo or the dialects of New Guinea. But I do believe that a part of our responsibility as stewards of the word is to make some sustained effort to step outside of our own linguistic comfort zone and really learn another language — not only for purposes of comporting ourselves respectably abroad, but much more importantly, to stay in contact with the complicating alternatives to our own linguistic window on the world and, by doing so, to cultivate the humility required to use words generously and well.

George Steiner, who is himself conversant with at least fifteen languages, makes the simple claim that "The poly-glot is a freer man" (or woman, I would add).[3] Study of languages and of the structures of language as a whole branch of philosophy lie at the heart of liberal education — the learning designed to free us from dangerous parochialism.

I don't know when parochialism and insularity have been more dangerous than they are now. Given the global crises that make transnational cooperation more imper-ative than ever, any of us who can find our way into alter-native cultural points of view need to do so and to modify an entrenched imperial discourse of paternalism and

3. George Steiner, *Real Presences* (Chicago: University of Chicago Press, reprint edition, 1991), p. 57.

control by modeling authentic multicultural awareness. Many of our ambassadors cannot speak the languages of the countries to which they are sent. This should embarrass us. It should also motivate us to be ambassadors where we can, and to consider carefully what is gained in translation, not only into English, but in the effort it takes to move out of English into another environment of thought and feeling.

One of the exercises I do in poetry courses that has proven exhilarating every time is to hand out and read aloud poems in French, German, and Spanish. Only those who don't know the language in question may participate in discussion of the poem. The object is to consider how much may be understood without specific understanding of the denotative content of the words on the page — how much of our understanding may come from sound values, musicality, rhythm, and structure. Somehow students pick up the gentle melancholy and mood of reverie in these lines from Appolinaire: "Sous le pont Mirabeau coule la Seine,/et nos amours, faut-il qu'il m'en souvienne,/la joie venait toujours après la peine./Vienne la nuit, sonne l'heure/les jours s'en vont, je demeure."[4] Or the sense of something dwindling toward loss in Rilke's "Herbsttag":

---

4. Guillaume Appolinaire, "Sous le pont Mirabeau," in *Alcools* (Paris: Klincksieck, 1997).

Wer jetzt kein Haus hat, baut sich keines mehr.
Wer jetzt allein ist, wird es lange bleiben,
Wird wachen, lesen, lange Briefe schreiben,
Und wird in den Alleen hin und her unruhig
    wandern,
Wenn die Blätter treiben.[5]

Simply to hear the sounds of another language can be a salutary reminder of the limitations of our own. That we separate events into subjects and objects with a verb in between; that we partition time with both simple and perfect tenses; that we still, transformational grammar notwithstanding, commonly think in terms of eight parts of speech but fudge the categories with participles and gerunds; that we have prepositions like "of" that do the work of several but evade easy definition — all signify peculiar ways in which we have adapted the sensations and impressions that run along our nerves and hum in our brains to an architecture that resembles something grand and Gothic, not altogether practical, but offering commodious space for habitation. Still, there are connections that can be made in Russian that English speakers cannot altogether fathom, and metaphors available in Basque and Finnish and Japanese to which we have no immediate access.

5. Rainer Maria Rilke, "Herbsttag," in *The Selected Poetry of Rainer Maria Rilke,* ed. and trans. Stephen Mitchell (New York: Vintage Books, 1989).

We do, however, have mediated access to them if we are willing to be taught. Even to learn a few phrases of another language is to receive a gift and open a door of diplomacy and, more importantly, of mutual goodwill. Such efforts are the more urgent as this country becomes increasingly multilingual and as the global community stands in ever more urgent need of mutual understanding. As John McWhorter reminds us, "For a vast proportion of Americans now and surely for a good long time beyond, English will be a language they had to work to learn and never spoke perfectly, or a language that they grew up with in school but did not use in the home with their closest intimates during their formative years."[6] In Santa Barbara, where I have spent the last twelve years, about 42 percent of the local population speak Spanish as a first language. In Los Angeles County, public school district teachers are trying to accommodate upwards of fifty-five different language groups. This is a problem and a challenge, but also an invigorating opportunity to open up a cultural awareness that has been deeply affected — not to say afflicted — by isolationism and unhealthy delusions of hegemony.

American monolingualism continues a historical attitude of imperialism and privilege that is increasingly

6. John McWhorter, *Doing Our Own Thing: The Degradation of Language and Music and Why We Should, Like, Care* (New York: Gotham, reprint edition, 2004), p. 234.

dangerous in a world where the deep differences between large populations involved in mutual distrust and fear of large-scale violence threaten all our peace. If we are to be peacemakers, we need to cross language barriers wherever we can — and if we can't personally make that journey, we need to support vigorously efforts to build a critical mass of people who can do so through education, travel, and incentives for adults working in cross-cultural environments. Curiously, such efforts are often quite controversial. That all students in California — a state where well over a third of the population is native Spanish speakers — learn basic Spanish is controversial. Many of them are (and arguably "should" be) bilingual. But the question seems slow to follow: Why shouldn't native English speakers also be bilingual? Insistence on an official language has its rationale, partly economic, since the mere business of posting dual-language road signs, as any resident of Quebec will attest, creates a significant dent in the provincial budget. But single-language policy helps to maintain class segregation and forfeits the richness of intercultural contact to which we give a good deal of lip service.

Engagement in learning foreign languages also serves to make the logic of our own language world and many of our imbedded assumptions more visible. We are brought to terms with our own terms in a new way. And we become aware of an important dimension of vocation, which is to learn ways to bridge the gaps that keep us separate and suspicious — to "mind the gap," if you will!

Learning a language also sensitizes us to the various filters through which history and culture come to us. That English is not God's native language is an important piece of news that a few people haven't quite registered yet. The church would do well to deliver that news in any number of ways — for instance, by sharing space with congregations who speak other languages, or by introducing hymns and some programming that serve both to remind us of the larger ecclesial body and to acculturate us to the environment in which many of our brothers and sisters worship. Occasional bilingual readings in congregations where some portion of the people come from a different language group are another simple possibility, if only for the sake of raising mutual awareness.

In congregations where English is the only language, regular focus on the differences among English translations of Scripture can offer lively opportunities to reflect on the complex way that the biblical story comes to us — filtered through multiple translations, each of which carries its own theological emphasis, many of which were undertaken and completed (like Tyndale's) in highly politically charged environments where not only theological issues but issues of state authority were at stake. For those who haven't yet seen it, I recommend David Daniell's *The Bible in English* — for a detailed, copious, but very readable chronicle of that history.[7] I also can't recommend highly enough George Steiner's "Preface to the Hebrew Bible" for its insightful account of the legacy those successive translations constitute.[8]

The history of the Bible in English offers a fascinating study of how highly politicized, fraught with special interest, and riddled with ambiguities is the business of translation, and how consequential. Of course the Bible is a special case, but it offers translation issues that concern us all — even those who don't routinely read it. The mere fact that there are over seventy-five translations still available in English invites comparison and some reflection on what difference the differences make. Certainly the difference between "Thou shalt not kill" and "Thou shalt not commit murder," over which the translating team of the NRSV evidently had quite spirited discussion, offers an obvious case in point, pertinent in significant ways to the current political issues that divide us most sharply. Clearly, translating teams dealing with sacred texts bear heavy responsibilities.

But the equally obvious fact remains that the Spirit works in and through every one of those translations — the flawed, the inaccurate, the unpoetic. Chana Bloch, a fine translator and poet who co-translated a beautiful

7. David Daniell, *The Bible in English: Its History and Influence* (New Haven: Yale University Press, 2003).

8. George Steiner, "A Preface to the Hebrew Bible," in *No Passion Spent* (New Haven: Yale University Press, 1996).

and lively new translation of the Song of Songs in 1998,[9] pointed out to me both infelicities and inaccuracies in the King James Version with which I grew up and which I still revere for its dignity and standard-setting English lines. I read those with a different sense of their value now, not exactly diminished but modified. What such comparisons and revaluations continue to teach me is that there is grace in variation, grace in the process, that efforts to find ways faithfully to render the sacred story will be blessed. Each time a translator picks up the ancient texts, God puts God's word and self once again in human hands and submits to our care. That, in itself, is worth a good deal of reflection: while we see through a glass darkly, we receive all that we can know through the filters of human discourse, and yet the one who is living Truth manages to keep offering and maintaining relationship with us. Words are instrumental and essential to the relationship, but malleable, inherently ambiguous, mere images and shadows of divine things.

Does this mean that precision doesn't matter? No. Does it mean that we need not be concerned about flaws and imprecisions in the translations we read, insofar as we are able to recognize them? Certainly not. Indeed, those who have the training to make those discernments offer an invaluable service to the rest of us who never

9. Chana and Ariel Bloch, trans., *The Song of Songs* (Berkeley and Los Angeles: University of California Press, 1998).

darkened the door of a Hebrew class. Some translations diminish the light of the Word. Some are luminous with original energy. Which translations of Scripture we use as worshiping communities and as individuals make a difference in how we define and develop our relationships with God and each other. To the extent of our literacy, we are responsible for choosing the text that keeps us most mindful of God's mystery and sovereignty, and keeps our hearts most open to the mysterious whisperings of the Spirit as they reach us through these heavily edited, much mediated texts.

Though Scripture is a special case, it can serve to keep us attentive to and aware of how wisdom may come from many places if we are willing to work at the linguistic boundaries where veils need respectfully to be lifted — or where sometimes walls must fall. Cynthia Ozick, a translator and a poet, makes this observation about the work of faithful translation: "When we read a poem in translation, we want to feel we are reading the poem itself. We do not want to feel suspicious or unsure. We want to hand ourselves over to the given-ness of the poem, and to rest in the authority of its being."[10]

So, she suggests, it is at those boundaries that something emerges which is neither wholly original nor wholly derivative, but the fruit of a rich partnership that

10. Cynthia Ozick, *Metaphor and Memory* (New York: Vintage Books, reprint edition, 1991), p. 200.

involves both the translator and those who read the work in translation in a certain creative tension. That creative tension invites every reader to enter into the business of translation as a third partner, taking the measure of differences and distances where possible.

We are all called into partnerships of this kind. We are called to be translators not only from one spoken language to another when we are able, but, perhaps more realistically for most of us, from one realm of discourse to another. Imagine a world where social scientists and literary scholars could converse together in mutual comprehension! Those of us in the professions have, I think, a serious obligation to make our work accessible and helpful to those outside them, and to enlarge discussions of professional issues in ways that enable wider reflection.

Think, for instance, of the specialized terms and processes involved in understanding the stem-cell debate. To make its complexities sufficiently understood for the public to be meaningfully involved in policymaking is not only a matter of biological education, but also a matter of attending to the character of the conversation that needs to be had. That is a translation project. Similarly, the vocabulary of economics needed to follow (and perhaps challenge) the activities of the World Bank or the World Trade Organization is basic equipment for serious participation in political process and change. Not that such understanding can be purveyed by means of a vocabulary list, but the most technical terms do have definitions that are capable of being rendered comprehensibly, and the more dangerous nontechnical terms like "healthy economy" and "privatization" and "growth" demand the ongoing examination due to any highly manipulable or euphemistic terms. So I hope in our various venues we can all bring our attention faithfully to the business of finding ways to define and articulate the concepts and processes that matter to us all. I hope we honor the simple question "What does that mean?" whenever it comes up, and encourage everyone in our communities of work and worship to ask it early and often.

Having urged accessibility, let me speak from the other side of my mouth for just a moment about the value of formality in speech. The beauty of a good translation of the Bible or of Tolstoy or of Rilke is indisputably a gift to the reader. So also it is a gift, rather against the American grain, to maintain — or perhaps at this stage, reintroduce — a respect for formal language. It might sound elitist to suggest such a thing, though John McWhorter, who fully affirms the value of "black English" and other forms of nonstandard speech that arise authentically from the needs and invention of living communities responding to their own expressive needs, maintains that formal or "high" language is by no means restricted to literate societies. "It requires no schoolrooms or textbooks. It is a general feature of being human."[11] To the extent that Americanization involves flattening or homogenizing social discourse to the lowest common denominator of formality, we sustain a loss of distinctions that have helped to maintain respect for elders, the stages of intimacy, the dignity of ritual occasions, and the beauty of oratory of the kind we remember from Martin Luther King Jr. Indeed, African-American churches are one of the places where such respect for the clarity and vitality of oratory is still widely practiced.

Of course, the issue of formal speech is fraught with class issues that demand particular sensitivity of those who work in the church. The historical class-based differences among American denominations are hard to talk about, but the influence of those distinctions lingers in the language that is used about worship and in worship, and has important implications for both evangelism and ecumenism. I cannot undertake here a detailed analysis of the complexities of denominational discourse, though it deserves at least a chapter in its own right. I simply suggest that among the practices that separate us, sometimes painfully, are the particular uses of words in worship. Arguments for and against liturgical formality are not to be trivialized.

The preservation of formal speech — a kind of liturgical sensibility extended into a wider realm — is related to the translation issues I've been citing because to craft a

11. McWhorter, *Doing Our Own Thing,* p. 37.

formal address engages one in so similar a process of re-thinking the finding of adequate equivalencies, concen-trating on the relative value of alternative ways of putting things. This engagement with words and meanings for the sake of calling one another into a richer, more toler-ant, and more inclusive community can be, in itself, a dis-cipline that sharpens the mind and opens the heart.

I remember being amused one time at a student's com-ment after several successive days devoted to Mary Oli-ver's poems. He asked, "Does she ever write about any-thing but death and transformation?" I had to think a minute. Then I realized the answer was "What else is there?" As a dear friend of mine once put it, "There are really only three great themes: freedom, power, and love." Prophecy is about the relationship among those three. Poetry finds ways to articulate that relationship. Transla-tion gives us shared access to the prophecies and the po-etry we need. And love is the energy that fuels the whole enterprise of wrestling with words and meanings.

Play

If any among you has not heard the BBC radio program "My Word," I urge you to hasten home and check your broadcast schedules, find their airtime, hunker down with a cup of tea, and enjoy word sport of the wittiest kind. True and false etymologies are made equally entertaining; curious word specimens are retrieved from the darker corners of the dictionary to be made the subject of sharp wit; and spontaneous shaggy-dog puns elevate that much-abused art form into admirable respectability. High intelligence engaged in word play offers not only entertainment but encouragement. Because to play with words is to love them, delight in them, honor their possibilities, and take them seriously. Real play engages what matters. Wordplay is the basis of both good poetry and clear thought. Storytelling is rooted in the spirit of play. As Barry Sanders puts it, every telling of a story "dances and sports with reality in order to coax and tease a brand-new world out into the open." He goes on to remind us of Ezra Pound's coining of the term *logopoeia* —

"the dance of the intellect among words" — a term and an idea that point back to an ancient Greek inscription, "Who now of all dancers sports most playfully."[1] So I want to recommend logopoeia as a valuable and necessary stewardship practice.

But first, let's consider for a few moments the general value of play. I began to rethink my ideas about work and play some years ago when a student gave me a book by jazz musician Stephen Nachmanovitch called *Free Play: The Power of Improvisation in Life and the Arts.*[2] Or perhaps my rethinking dates back much further to the time when my daughters were little and I read the works of Maria Montessori, the pioneering educator who founded the Montessori schools. Both Nachmanovitch and Montessori overturn the very common idea in this culture that children play and adults work. Montessori's great contribution to early childhood education was to understand children's play as work — the arduous, serious, methodical, purposeful, deep work of establishing patterns in the body and mind that will serve as templates for all further learning. Nachmanovitch's timely message to adults in a post-industrial, fast-paced, productivity-focused, time-driven culture is that some of the most important activity of adult life is play. The real

1. Barry Sanders, *A Is for Ox* (New York: Pantheon Books, 1994), p. 80.

2. Stephen Nachmanovitch, *Free Play: Improvisation in Life and Art* (Los Angeles: Jeremy Tarcher, 1990).

leaders — the people who recall us to our deepest purposes and model fruitful lives — are people who know how to play.

The kind of play I'm speaking of is childlike, not childish. If we are to accept the invitation to "become like little children" in order to enter the Kingdom of Heaven, we need to understand how to retrieve what is truly and essentially childlike while resisting temptations to waste time on what is childish. It's not so easy. The deep engagement characteristic of child's play is generally defeated by multiple electronic and commercial distractions in this culture at an early age, and we have to work to retrieve it. Sadly, academic institutions too often discourage the free play of the mind, much as, individually, we all may and should encourage it.

It troubles me to think how frequently I encounter anxiety in students who would like to take risks and try new ways of reading or writing, find their own voices, put a metaphoric spin on a sentence, or indulge in a colorful digression, but don't do it because they "need an A" to maintain a scholarship or stay on the team or stay in school. Or simply because, somewhere, someone drowned curiosity in pedantry. Play, alas, is a dimension of learning that has been trained out of far too many young people by the time they reach college. I say this on the unscientific basis of my own observations in almost thirty years of teaching. The rigor and earnestness and grim determination to do the right thing that many "good" students bring to the classroom are heartbreaking.

Certainly correctness matters. Clarity, organization, disciplined argumentation, precise word choice, factual accuracy — all these things matter. But to transpose a thought from Saint Paul, if one has all these things and has not love, it profits him nothing. Which brings me to my next point about play.

Play comes from loving life, and play with words comes from loving language. Montaigne, one of the more playful writers I encountered in my arduous years as a French major, coined the term *essai* (which simply means an attempt or a trial) for the little thought pieces that have since become a genre unto themselves. His writing has the delightful exuberance of someone who went through life saying, in effect, like E. M. Forster, "How can I tell what I think till I see what I say?"[3] Writing, for him, was a way of thinking aloud and trying things out.

The idea of writing as a process of playing around with words gets lost in environments where writing is so frequently treated as a commodity. In the face of deadlines, word counts, and resumés to fatten, ten blank pages don't readily present themselves to the imagination as play space. So, as a writing instructor who wants to encourage fruitful play, I look for language that might

3. E. M. Forster, *Aspects of the Novel* (London: Edward Arnold, Abinger edition, 1974).

restore vitality to the process. "Play with this idea. See where it takes you. Give it a shot. See how many ways of putting it you can come up with. Try it out. Spin it out. Play it out. See how it feels." The point about feeling brings me to another important part of work as play.

I'm amazed at how many people I encounter seem to have been taught to dismiss their feelings when they read or write or work at solving problems. At the risk of reinforcing the damaging stereotype that humanities types are a touchy-feely lot, unlike their brethren in the "hard" sciences, I will admit that I myself practice literary criticism by doing unabashedly what I often must persuade hesitant students to do, which is to put feeling first: to start my analysis of the work in question with where and what it made me feel — anything: outrage, compassion, amusement, confusion, or even boredom. The phrase I just used was coined by E. E. Cummings: "since feeling is first,/who pays any attention/to the syntax of things/will never wholly kiss you . . ."[4] I don't literally believe that; I pay attention to the syntax of things and certainly take due pleasure in kisses and other nonintellectual pursuits. But in a certain unavoidable way, feeling *is* first. We don't go around having ideas. We go around gathering impressions, sensations, feelings, absorbing a mishmash of

4. E. E. Cummings, "Since feeling is first," in *E. E. Cummings: Complete Poems, 1914-1962,* ed. George J. Firmage (New York: Liveright, 1991), p. 291.

stimuli which, when stirred properly, eventually resolves into ideas. To start in the place of feeling is to enter the task of interpretation, analysis, composition, or problem-solving at the point of highest available energy. What is felt, in the body, in the heart, fuels the intellect.

So a playful approach to *Hamlet* might begin with questions that come from felt response. Why was Hamlet so obnoxious to Ophelia when she hadn't done anything to him? What's going on between him and his mother? Why am I so moved when he and Laertes both figure out they've been had? The felt questions are also the serious questions that lead into the deepest intricacies of the playwright's craft and the human psyche — Hamlet's and Shakespeare's and our own. As one of my favorite characters in another play proclaims, "I am interested in my feelings!" And so ought we all to be. They are the soil from which thought springs.

Once the thought has sprung, it seems, the work begins. And here's where we get serious about staying playful. There's a certain kind of determination that sets in when one has drafted a thesis sentence and shored it up with an outline or embarked upon an argument in a public forum or mapped out a plan for a project. Suddenly what was once a living, pulsing idea is locked behind a grid, in the grim hope that it will stay still and submit quietly to the terms of imprisonment for the duration of the task. A grisly metaphor, I grant you, but you should hear the language that some students use about the business of literary analysis. I quote from recent memory — I kid you not. "I've tried to tear apart this poem, but I just can't get much out of it." "We learned to dissect poetry in high school, but I never liked doing it much." Or worse, "When you get down to what the poet's trying to say, it's that life is hard [or sad, or a bowl of cherries]" — as though the "life" of the poem is right down there with the dregs in the bottom of the wine bottle. It reminds me of a cartoon I had on my office door for a while that I finally took down in fear that someone might take it seriously. A reader looking up from a book comments, "Take away all the poetic language, and he's just some depressed guy." The students I continue to usher through the dark labyrinths of Eliot's *Waste Land* may well wonder how to play in the brambly thickets of those pages. The play they offer has to be done in the dark; it takes a long time to "get" *The Waste Land,* but along the way, if you consent to the terms of the poem, it is possible to enjoy — even in the midst of portents and loss — the rich play of words. And this brings me to another point about play.

Play involves risk and trust: consent to the possibility of failure, consent to act with imperfect data or incomplete information. It's a commonplace worth remembering that we succeed only to the extent that we're willing to risk failure. I think of David and Peter — two of my favorite characters in the Bible. Both of them had a kind of audacity, spontaneity, and even playfulness that led them to great risks, great failures, and finally great lives of faith. Think of Peter leaping out of the boat to run and meet Jesus on the water. What a stupendous act of trust and self-forgetfulness that was. Peter's trust faltered, but those first few steps out on the water must have been a moment of wild play and shocking revelation to him.

So what does it mean, practically speaking, to act in trust? On a psychological level, it means to pay attention to intuition, to the nonrational hunches that come unbidden as little gifts from the unconscious mind, which we can trust as a rich repository of all we have learned and which will prove to us time and again that we know more than we think we do. It is to trust in the truth that we are saved, loved, and perfectly safe, and so we are free to play around a little. Consider, for example, the role of trust in sports. In swimming, you have to learn to let go of the side of the pool. In skiing, you have to yield to the force of gravity. In surfing, you have to submit to the power and direction of the wave. In basketball, you have to decide when to pass and when to make the shot. In baseball, you gauge when to steal a base. Skill at any sport requires flexibility and the ability to adjust to shifting circumstances immediately — and this includes, of course, the skill of using words well.

Flexibility requires permission. One cannot be playful if one does not feel wholly and wholeheartedly permitted to be so. That permission comes most deeply from the conviction that one is loved, that the play will be rewarded, that what we call failure is an essential part of the process. It is the attitude that allowed Chesterton to proclaim that "If it's worth doing, it's worth doing badly," and Auden to advise that you "Leap before you look." It lies behind paradoxes like "Make haste slowly" and "When you're hanging on for dear life, let go." The feeling that we are permitted to play allows us to let go of outcomes — a basic teaching of most wisdom traditions — and to receive the promptings of the Spirit, who moves within us and among us to ends we cannot and need not foresee. It was surely in this spirit that Jesus advised the disciples as he sent them forth: "And when they bring you before the synagogues and the rulers and the authorities, do not be anxious how or what you are to answer or what you are to say; for the Holy Spirit will teach you in that very hour what you ought to say" (Luke 12:11-12, RSV).

To play is to claim our freedom as beloved children of God and to perform our most sacred tasks — what we feel we are called to do in the world — with abandon and delight, free to experiment and fail, free to find out and reconsider, free to say something we might need to take back, free to look stupid in the interests of honesty because there are no grades and, as my husband often kindly reminds me, "There is no competition in the Kingdom of Heaven." Children who feel completely safe and loved are playful. To play is to live in grace. And to live in grace is not to ignore the law — there must be a lucid thesis sentence, and comma splices must be eschewed — but to embrace it as an aid to an abundant life. So, in the interests of abundant life, good stewards play. Let me offer two brief examples of the kind of play that revitalizes the words we use and the wit it takes to use them well. The first is a passage from *Traveling Mercies,* Anne Lamott's remarkably frank story of a faith journey from utter squalor to a life of gratitude and productive wordplay. One particular day, she wakes up with a vicious headache and asks a neighbor with cancer to do her a favor:

> I hate being the kind of person who tries to get someone with stage-four metastatic lung cancer to feel sorry for her just because she has a headache. (Though it *was* an ice-pick headache.) But the way I see things, God loves you the same whether you're being elegant or not. It feels much better when you are, but even when you can't fake it, God still listens to your prayers. . . .
>
> Again and again I tell God I need help, and God says, "Well, isn't that fabulous? Because I need help too. So you go get that old woman over there some water, and I'll figure out what we're going to do about *your* stuff."[5]

5. Anne Lamott, *Traveling Mercies: Some Thoughts on Faith* (New York: Random House, 2000), p. 120.

What seems to me most striking about Lamott's free-wheeling, think-out-loud style is the permission she gives herself — or receives — to barge across the boundaries of decorum for a good cause. Her theology and her writing — both of which she takes completely seriously — are playful. She allows herself to be straightforward, to reach for odd similes, to indulge in quirky allusions, to put lung cancer in a sentence that turns out to be funny, to write down a shoot-from-the-hip dialogue with God. She often appropriates current slang ("Don't get me wrong: grief sucks," she insists later after she offers several vivid images to get at what grief feels like), but she does so in a way that allows us to laugh with her at its inadequacies. She considers how Jesus' admonition to give a cup of water to those who thirst might play out on an ordinary day — and goes directly to where her imagination takes her. What she gets to in the course of her emotionally complex, wide-ranging conversion narrative is a chronicle of grace and mercy as eloquent in its way as Bunyan's *Grace Abounding to the Chief of Sinners.*

Lamott's playfulness is largely a matter of stance, tone, and attitude. If we reach back a little further and look at the poetry and prose of E. E. Cummings, we find a different kind of playfulness that is more exclusively and specifically verbal. Consider, for instance, this passage from *Six Nonlectures* in which he recalls his childhood home in Cambridge:

The servants — and this strikes me as a more than important point — very naturally enjoyed serving: for they were not ignobly irresponsible impersons, they were not shamelessly overpaid and mercilessly manipulated anonymities, they were not pampered and impotent particles of a greedy and joyless collective obscenity. In brief: they were not slaves. Actually, these good and faithful servants (of whom I speak) were precisely everything which no slave can ever be — they were alive; they were loved and loving human beings. From them, a perfect ignoramus could and did learn what any unworld will never begin to so much as suspect: that slavery, and the only slavery, is service without love.[6]

The characteristic coinages we learned to recognize in his poetry (remember "puddlewonderful" and the "leaping greenly spirits of trees") appear here in "impersons" and "unworld," both of which startlingly underscore the point he's making about how service becomes degraded and dehumanized. It is a serious point, but not deadly serious — rather, it is a lively seriousness about something that Cummings grasps so thoroughly and sees so clearly that he can afford to be playful in his reflections about it. Because play comes from clarity and confi-

6. E. E. Cummings, *Six Nonlectures* (Cambridge: Harvard University Press, reprint, 1991), p. 26.

dence that knows it need not protect what cannot be destroyed.

We recognize playfulness that is rooted in serenity and surrender and undefensive openness of heart with particular piquancy in the poems of the haiku masters. In their hands, ordinary events witnessed with a childlike will to pleasure and readiness to be surprised are chronicled in lines that require only a breath to say but expand in the mind on ripples of laughter. Issa's gentle irreverence, for instance, reminds us of indecorous distractions that invade interior quiet and link us insistently to the mundane:

> Fleas, lice,
> a horse peeing
> near my pillow.

In his hands, a simple observation of a natural process is cause for delight:

> From all these trees,
> in the salads, the soup, everywhere
> cherry blossoms fall.

Small incongruities make comedy of the ordinary. And nature participates in that comedy as though at play with us:

> The clouds
> are giving these moon-watchers
> a little break.[7]

In haiku, poetry, play, and something very like prayer converge. Small events, observed with generous curiosity, yield epiphanies. The playful mind finds pleasure and wisdom lurking in the same hiding place, as we see in this unpublished haiku by James Liguri:

> Up through the surface
> of the old pond
> the eyes of a frog

> Into the old pond
> the frog jumps
> Splash!

These examples represent different forms of verbal playfulness, all of which may be helpful models of rhetorical alertness and proficiency. But in a wider sense, putting words together is inherently playful, because creation itself is play. (G. K. Chesterton, in his delightful little book *Orthodoxy,* imagines the act of creation as God at play. He considers a field of daisies and imagines

---

7. See *The Essential Haiku: Versions of Basho, Buson, and Issa,* ed. Robert Hass (Hopewell, N.J.: Ecco Press, 1994), pp. 39, 44, 36.

God, having created one daisy, delighted with it, saying to himself, "Do it again! Do it again!"[8]) Think of the high place given to words in our sacred tradition. At the beginning of John's Gospel we read, "In the beginning was the Word." The word with a small "w" is not unrelated to that Word, or to the Word made flesh. Poetry, even secular poetry, borders very closely on prayer insofar as it honors the life-giving power of the word. We have become desensitized, in ways discussed earlier, to the electrifying power of the well-chosen word. But sometimes it breaks through like a ray of light through a cloud bank. We all know the experience of reading or perhaps writing a sentence that evokes with absolute laser-like precision a particular feeling, atmosphere, action, or thought which, being named, seems to take on brand-new life. Even bleak images like Shakespeare's "bare ruin'd choirs" and Eliot's "fear in a handful of dust" offer sudden pleasure in their accuracy. In those moments we may recognize that the privilege given to Adam of naming the creatures of the earth is also given to us.

Reclaiming an appropriate practice of play is one of the challenges of adulthood. The grown-ups I most admire love wordplay, love the play of the mind, play with ideas, and lace their speech with images, metaphors,

8. G. K. Chesterton, *Orthodoxy* (San Francisco: Ignatius Press, reprint edition, 1995), p. 66.

comparisons, and recollections that invite others to play along. Such playfulness is a fruit of the Spirit, since as a quality of being and a habit of mind and speech, it is inseparable from so many other virtues — receptivity, openness of heart, trust, confidence, grace, even love.

The original charge of both the academy and the church was to be places that nurture the mind and the spirit. That mission involved both institutions deeply and consistently in producing and practicing poetry and in the play of the mind and imagination that required. For a good part of Western history, churchmen were expected and trained to be wordsmiths. What we see in the best of them — the theologians and the scholars, as well as the poets — is a capacity for play. Not humor — not always — though that is certainly one mark of the Spirit, but the receptive, intuitive readiness to recognize grace in any form and respond, the willingness both to obey and to suspend rules according to the demands of the situation — in a word, wit.

By and large, we have, as a culture, abandoned wit, with its high and demanding standards, for the lesser satisfactions of sarcasm, wry remarks, and ill-gotten punch lines. The British, alas, are following us on that downward path to intellectual sloth, but haven't yet completely forgotten Austen or Johnson or betrayed the trust of Shakespeare — who is, after all, their national treasure.

In the ancient, yellowing dictionary that sits in state

outside my office I look up *wit* and find a bit of gem-like musing worthy of England's best: "The faculty of associating ideas in a new and ingenious, as well as natural and pleasing, way: the felicitous combination of words and thoughts by which unexpected resemblances between things apparently unlike are vividly set before the mind so as to produce a shock of pleasant surprise. . . ." A good metaphor, it appears, is wit in action.

John Donne is the poet most closely associated with the particular notion of wit that prevailed in the lively literary circles of seventeenth-century London. Donne's metaphorical impulse seems almost manic; in some poems he pushes a metaphor as far as logic will take it and then moves on into fantasy, spinning it wildly into pun or paradox along the way. In an erotic poem to a mistress, he likens lovemaking to exploration in the exclamation, "Oh, my America! My new-found-land!" and proceeds to detail her hills and valleys with rakish relish, justifying a questionable alliance with the same arguments that sustained imperialism, suggesting, perhaps (wittily — miss the point if you will), something suspect in both applications of the argument.[9]

In some poems Donne multiplies metaphors, so that one "unexpected resemblance between things appar-

---

9. John Donne, "To His Mistress, Going to Bed," in *The Complete Poetry and Selected Prose of John Donne* (New York: Random House, Modern Library, 1952), p. 83.

ently unlike" follows another with disconcerting agility. In "Batter My Heart" (Holy Sonnet XIV), for instance, the heart of the sinner is likened first to a piece of metal in the hands of a smith, then to a town under seige, then to a woman given to an unworthy partner in marriage. Each image (breathlessly following the last) demands a particular line of theological reasoning; we are stopped short by myriad implications even as we're moved along on the momentum of the argument. And each challenges conventional, comforting ideas about God with ideas that restore tension, mystery, and strenuousness to the devotional life of the believer.[10] Reading Donne's poems is like entering an intellectual tennis match; shots come from unforeseen angles, accurate and graceful, and if you pick them up, you find yourself being accurate and graceful too.

That's the main delight of wit, it seems to me — that it's both challenging and inviting. In my encounters with truly witty people, I have come away gratified not only by displays of quick and quirky intelligence, but by the ways they invited and allowed me to rise to an unusual level of precision and surprise myself. One of my best tennis coaches was a high-school boyfriend who never played down to me. Though he was by far the better player and always won, and though I was sometimes (reasonably)

10. John Donne, "Batter My Heart," in *The Complete Poetry and Selected Prose of John Donne,* p. 252.

frustrated and annoyed at his insistence on playing his best even with so poor a partner, I played better tennis with him than with anyone who made more concessions. Meeting his shots, though I might succeed in doing so only infrequently, could be as satisfying as winning. Conversation with witty people can have the same effect. Their generosity consists not in concessions, but in the assumption that you can and will meet them on the court and do your part in a good and strenuous game.

Oscar Wilde's wit is probably better known than Donne's, if only because local theater companies still find so much to play with in his campy, late-Victorian farce, *The Importance of Being Earnest.* Known for the pithy epigrams that lace his letters, Wilde has left a legacy of tools for self-examination. Consider, for instance, this observation: "Women are always like their mothers; that is their tragedy. Men are never like their mothers, and that is theirs." Or the implications of the line he arrived at by inverting Aristotle's "Art imitates life" to offer an equally valuable insight: "Life imitates art." Guided, it seems, by the general principle that "The opposite is also true," he provided a whole generation with paradox enough to hoist itself by its own petard.

Much more ancient in the annals of English language and thought is a usage that links wit to conscience. A fourteenth-century poet, Michelis of Northgate, entitled his now-obscure treatise on remorse "The Ayenbyte of Inwit," which may be roughly translated as "the recurring bite of conscience." How lovely and vigorous an idea — to link the fine-tuned, quick, sharp-edged precision of wit with conscience — our faculty of self-knowing and moral reasoning, the voice of the best self. A conscience that acts as "inner wit" or "inwit" suggests a conscience that would never suffer a fool gladly, put up with self-serving rationalization, offer cheap grace, strain at gnats, or swallow camels. Wit, in this case, is the voice that says "Don't kid yourself" or "You knew better than that" or "Don't be so simple-minded." It is the champion of clarity, of what Adrienne Rich called "hard-won simplicity." The distiller of truth.

Distillation may be a good metaphor for the process by which a playful wit arrives at wisdom. Distillation steams away all that is not the essence. What is left is potent, pungent, intense, possibly poisonous, always dangerous in the wrong hands. Distillation doesn't squander. It saves what is precious and lets go what is not. Distillation takes time. Real wit waits. When the right moment comes, it makes its move, fully equipped, at full strength.

Wit doesn't argue with sophists, simpletons, or demagogues. It waves them on their downward path with a quip. They don't even know they've been had. Wit withers with a smile; it never wrangles; it prefers fine-pointed instruments to bludgeons, and uses them to more effect. It is well-read and borrows its best lines from the best sources. Wit lands lightly and leaves quickly, never explains a punch line or takes too long to deliver one. Wit knows its place in the service of what matters; its best performances support thoughtful argument, sober reflection, and poetic vision without upstaging them. Wit awakens the willing and ready and leaves sluggards to their sleep. It doesn't proselytize or preach, but it does speak truth to power, expose the hypocrite, and incite its victims to the distressing self-awareness they may have sought to avoid.

An expression I still hear now and then from one of my parents' generation — "It scared me out of my wits!" — implies something else about wit worth thinking about. It cannot co-exist or cooperate with fear. When we have our wits about us, we are capable of courage. When fear takes over, wit is tragically defeated. Wit sees a way and takes it, doesn't waste a moment in self-pity, sins boldly, and, as Luther also put it, believes more boldly still. Wit takes calculated risks, consenting to the costs. Perhaps we should hear the ancient admonition "Therefore, choose life" as a call to keep our wits about us. Wit serves life as fear serves death. It seems, in fact, not to stretch a point too far to suggest that wit is related not only to the moral faculty (as conscience), but to faith itself. Wit steps out on thin ice when there is something of value to be won. Wit relies on intuition, accepts mystery, expects and accepts grace, and laughs.

The voice of Wendell Berry's "Mad Farmer" admonishes us, "Laugh./Laughter is immeasurable. Be joyful/

though you have considered all the facts."[11] Wit acknowledges darkness, but chooses light. Its laughter never ignores evil, but defies it. It finds the exact leverage point needed to turn a tragic tale to a story of hope retrieved from the rubble. Those who escape by using their wits, the B'rer Rabbits of the battlefield, laugh, perhaps, in sheer astonishment that life comes on such complicated terms, with no instructions, riddled with potholes and pockmarks, and still we survive, and still have the will to find a fiddler on the roof and dance.

reminds me of Richard Marius's Awe

11. Wendell Berry, "The Mad Farmer: Liberation Front," in *Collected Poems of Wendell Berry, 1957-1982* (San Francisco: North Point Press, 1987), p. 151.

Pray

My favorite definition of prayer is "the practice of the presence of God" — that is, to dwell secure in knowing ourselves to be loved and to be in love — open toward God, oriented toward God, struggling with God sometimes, out of authentic longing for understanding and a right relation, and in conversation with him, bringing all that happens to us back into that conversation.

This practice serves our deepest needs, not God's. As Milton rightly pointed out, "God doth not need either man's work or his own gifts. . . ." He certainly doesn't need our words; we can speak to him in the utter simplicity of silence. But even in human relationship, love drives us to words, often to poetry. It impels us to seek language for what fills our hearts. As Wallace Stevens said about the work of poetry, "It has to find what will suffice." This is often, also, the work of prayer. Language crafted into poetry or prayer raises us out of one silence to the edge of another. Near that threshold where all words fail is where prayer and poetry often converge.

210

Pray

One of the core claims of George Steiner's long reflection on language and story, *Real Presences,* is that close engagement with words inevitably involves us in encounter with the divine. "Any coherent understanding of what language is and how language performs," he writes, "any coherent account of the capacity of human speech to communicate meaning and feeling is, in the final analysis, underwritten by the assumption of God's presence."[1] This extravagant claim takes an extraordinarily high view of language, as a gift from God that functions as a vehicle of grace and truth because God is its source. As Steiner continues, he reminds us of the great silence behind speech, the ways in which all language acts emerge from and return to a silence that is full, not empty, and persists in creative tension with the breaches of utterance. The language of prayer, in particular, enters into this silence as into sacred space, seeking not to break the silence but to inhabit it.

The story is told of Mother Teresa that when an interviewer asked her, "What do you say when you pray?" she answered, "I listen." The reporter paused a moment, then asked, "Then what does God say?" and she replied, "He listens."[2] It is hard to imagine a more succinct way to get at the intimacy of contemplative prayer. There is a di-

1. George Steiner, *Real Presences* (Chicago: University of Chicago Press, reprint edition, 1991), p. 3.

2. See Malcolm Muggeridge, *Something Beautiful for God* (San Francisco: Harper, 1986).

mension to prayer that is wordless: we know that beyond the reach of our imaginations and abilities, the Spirit "intercedes for us with groanings too deep for words" (Rom. 8:26). We know that God hears the inarticulate cries of those who have no words for their suffering or their gratitude or their rage.

Still, Jesus taught us to pray, and gave us words for that purpose. Christians receive and recite the Lord's Prayer as a good and sufficient prayer in itself and also as a template for the prayers we are moved to speak and write as life gives us circumstances that drive us to our knees. We have been invited into an ongoing conversation with God, and what we say matters. All the basic acts of communication — storytelling, public speaking, private conversation, the making of poetry — are at their roots related to prayer. In *Legends of Our Time,* Elie Wiesel writes that at the heart of every story is a song.[3] Similarly, we might say that every sentence derives its life from the original and deepest kind of utterance, which is prayer. Even the conventionalities we exchange are borne on the breath of life that is given to us for the ultimate purpose of finding our way into loving relationship with God and each other.

Having made such a comprehensive claim, I would hasten to qualify it by assuring alarmed readers that I do

3. Elie Wiesel, *Legends of Our Time* (New York: Schocken Books, reprint edition, 2004).

what prayer does

not believe all utterance is prayer. When we pray, we enter into a level of discourse that is set apart to serve our deepest purposes in mysterious and powerful ways that we cannot fully fathom. The words we use in prayer work to multiple purposes — to acknowledge God's presence to us, to invoke God's listening ear, to bring us into sacred time and space, to remind and instruct us, to give shape to intention, and, indeed, to transmit actual and efficacious love energy to those for whom we pray. So those words matter. To get at the ways they matter, we might consider singly two of the specific things that prayer does.

First, prayer reaffirms our relationship to God. Reaffirmation is both a "useless" (nonutilitarian) and a deeply useful kind of statement. To say, for instance, "You are the Almighty one" serves no informative purpose: we know what we are reaffirming, and certainly God knows. But to utter such words of acknowledgment, belief, and love, as the psalmist does so often, is to reclaim and root ourselves in our place on earth and in heaven. The words themselves effect that relocation. They bring us back from the places to which we have wandered. Such reminding literally re-organizes our minds, bringing them back from distraction and confusion to a focus that aligns us with God's purposes. It attunes us to the ways in which we are continually being addressed by the Spirit who guides us. Reaffirmations can be found in the prayers of every liturgical tradition. There is this declaration from the *Te Deum:* "Thou art the King of glory, O Christ. Thou art the everlasting Son of the Father." There is this observation from the Presbyterian *Book of Common Worship:* "Holy God, you see us as we are, and know our inmost thoughts." And there is this address from the prayer of a seventeenth-century reformer: "My Lord and my God, the only good and only worthy to be beloved with all the heart and soul . . ." Reaffirming central truths about who God is frames and focuses prayer, so that subsequent acts of confession, petition, and thanksgiving do not degenerate into mere self-therapeutic gestures.

Reaffirmation may include not only acknowledgment of who God is, but also review of God's promises that are the context in which we pray. So, for instance, one of Evelyn Underhill's prayers begins, "O Blessed Jesu Christ, who didst bid all who carry heavy burdens to come to thee, refresh us with thy presence and thy power."[4] Again, the act of reaffirmation serves not to remind the Lord of his promises, but to orient or locate us in right relationship to the one who has set the terms on which we can make any claims at all on the God of the Universe. The Presbyterian Book of Order offers these words about prayer: "In prayer, through the Holy Spirit, people . . . remember God's gra-

4. Evelyn Underhill, in *The Oxford Book of Prayer,* ed. George Appleton (New York: Oxford University Press, 1985), p. 122.

cious acts. . . ." Remembering literally puts back together what may have been dissipated or diffused by daily distractions.

Just as we remind ourselves of who God is, so we include in prayer words that remind us of who we are. Acts of corporate confession begin with acknowledgment of our essential sinfulness and need, the ways we are dependent on God's grace and mercy. Here again, utterance is not informative but performative: spoken confession releases us into forgiveness. Speaking enacts the attitude of repentance that is the precondition of healing and restoration. Like the naming of God's attributes and promises in praise, the particularity and specificity of what is named accounts for much of the psychological efficacy of confession. Consider how some of the standard liturgical formulas for confession provide vivid reminders of the nature of sin in the images they invoke. "We have erred and strayed in our ways like lost sheep . . ." offers an almost comical vision of sin as hapless stupidity, dependence, and even vulnerability to forces of evil we cannot defeat without God's help. "We have done what we ought not to have done, we have left undone what we ought to have done, and there is no health in us" reminds us to consider both commission and omission and the pervasive character of sinfulness, lest we be tempted to reserve some place of self-justification in the process of confession. Or consider the little inventory in this confession, written for the Church of Scotland:

God of mercy and of grace,
you know the secrets of our hearts:
how blind we are to our own faults,
yet harsh in judging others;
how swift we are to take for gain,
yet slow to give for others;
how proud we are of our successes,
yet grudging in our praise of others.[5]

The poetic parallels reinforce the perverseness of our self-protections and the ways in which, on every count, we deflect and project awareness of our own sins in order to preserve a comfortable unawareness rather than seeking real healing.

One last example suggests how a well-chosen metaphor may open the resistant imagination to the character of sin: "My soul is empty and barren, or if there be any treasure in it, it is but as a treasure locked up in some chest whose key is lost, when it should be opened for the use of others."[6] The image itself offers a way to pursue healing. Unlocking what is locked, opening what is closed, sharing rather than hoarding — all direct us to specific modes of action and correction.

There is, of course, a dark side to the relationship

5. See *Prayers from the Reformed Tradition: In the Company of a Great Cloud of Witnesses,* ed. Diane Karay Tripp (Louisville, Ky.: Witherspoon Press, 2001), p. 39.

6. John Flavel, in *Prayers from the Reformed Tradition,* p. 28.

with God — where acceptance of mystery gives way to doubt, where suffering becomes nearly unbearable in its inexplicability, and where the God of self-revelation seems overtaken by the God of self-concealment. This, too, needs to be — and has been — given words. Some of the most remarkable prayers in the legacy of liturgy and literature are arguments with God, the best of them strenuous, bold, and even brash with the presumption of children who take on parents in unequal battle, somehow knowing themselves to be held safe even as they flail and rage. Gerard Manley Hopkins's "Thou Art Indeed Just, Lord" offers a memorable and complex example of words that give shape to such an argument and provide a path through the thicket of despair:

> Thou art indeed just, Lord, if I contend
> With thee; but, sir, so what I plead is just.
> Why do sinners' ways prosper? and why must
> Disappointment all I endeavor end?
> Wert thou my enemy, O thou my friend,
> How wouldst thou worse, I wonder, than thou dost
> Defeat, thwart me? Oh, the sots and thralls of lust
> Do in spare hours more thrive than I that spend,
> Sir, life upon thy cause. See, banks and brakes
> Now leavèd how thick! lacèd they are again
> With fretty chervil, look, and fresh wind shakes
> Them; birds build — but not I build; no, but strain,

Time's eunuch, and not breed one work that wakes.
Mine, O thou lord of life, send my roots rain.[7]

The complex mix of tonalities in this prayer, beginning
with the playful "sir" in the opening address, moving into
the almost whining rhetorical questions and evidence of
unfair frustrations, and ending in a final petition that be-
speaks ultimate trust, testifies richly to the way words
work as stepping-stones through confusion to resolution.
What begins as argument ends in an act of vulnerability
and self-yielding. The words we encounter along the way
— *just, contend, plead, disappointment, friend* — offer
stopping points for reflection upon our paradoxical situation before God: familiar and strange, bound by law and
freed by grace, fulfilling and frustrating, longing satisfied.

And here's a second thing to consider about verbal prayer:
It reasserts the gift character of all we encounter and possess. Naming the circumstances and relationships in our
lives as gifts casts them in a new light. An inventory of specific blessings literally transforms the character of simple
events and encounters. A lovely prayer of the Presbyte-
rians of the Republic of Vanuatu, for instance, seems to
revel in simple enumeration of particular blessings, nam-

7. Gerard Manley Hopkins, "Thou Art Indeed Just, Lord," in *Poems
and Prose of Gerard Manley Hopkins,* ed. W. H. Gardner (Baltimore:
Penguin Books, 1961), p. 67.

ing each of the goods of daily life as a way of accepting
them from the hand of a provident God:

> We thank you, Lord God, for all your blessings to us:
>> Blessings of rain that make the trees around us,
>>> big and small,
>> Grass for our cattle,
>> Fruit trees and vegetables for our health.
> And for all our coconuts, cocoa, coffee, kava, and
>> cattle,
>> Which bring us prosperity.
>> We thank you for our daily food,
>> For manioc, taro, yam, kumala, banana, breadfruit,
>> and rice,
>> Which gives us power.
>> We thank you, Lord, for our meat,
>> For beef, pork, goat, chicken,
>> For fish in the sea,
>> Shellfish on reefs,
> Coconut crabs that live in the rocks.
>> We thank you for your gift of love:
>> For husbands and wives,
>> For the gift of children,
>> For homes, for families,
>> And for friends.[8]

8. See *Prayers from the Reformed Tradition,* p. 101.

The act of praying in this way, listing and naming, pausing over each blessing, allows us to re-awaken to the relational character of our lives in Christ, to the dynamic of grace in what we call happenstance, and to the abundance of divine attention made manifest in the "ordinary." To name is to recognize; and this re-cognition opens our minds and hearts to receive what we need once again and allow ourselves to be blessed.

The language of prayer, then, works on multiple levels. It reminds, reframes, and re-awakens; it humbles us and also empowers us to claim and act on God's promises; it brings our intentions into sharp focus; it engenders intimacy with God and also brings us into alignment, harmony, and unity with the other members of the Body of Christ and with the communion of saints and angels. When we "gather together to ask the Lord's blessing," the words we speak in one chorus literally bind us into that one Body.

There is room in the life of prayer for lively experimentation — permission to play in the fields of the Lord with words, crafted, borrowed, and bent to the purpose, that help us to sustain the conversation that sustains us in life. Beyond that, prayer, as we utter it, changes us. As Elizabeth O'Connor reminds us, "When the mystics speak of prayer, they are talking about that which will create in us a new structure of consciousness."[9]

9. Elizabeth O'Connor, *The Search for Silence* (Waco, Tex.: Word Books, 1972), p. 9.

Sometimes a single word, as in the practice of "centering prayer," can lift us into sacred encounter. Sometimes words received from another culture or generation can enlarge our sense of solidarity with the whole Body. Sometimes the prayers sung in hymns and psalms, adding the dimension of melody to our words, literalize the effort to come into harmony with those who, invisibly, sing continual praise. In spoken prayer we enter into a rich conversation with God, with ourselves, with those with whom we pray, with those for whom we pray, and, we can assume, also with those for whom our words may do work we neither know nor consciously intend. We cannot know the full extent of the work in which we participate, only that the words we utter in prayer are not breathed in vain but are borne on that breath of life like seeds on the wind, to flourish where the Spirit plants them.

The words of prayer work self-reflexively as well, to quiet the mind, to open the heart, and to shape our interior spaces into temples for the Holy Spirit. They are never adequate, though the least intention to pray will be received and made sufficient. In "Footnote to All Prayers," C. S. Lewis wisely concedes how even our praying words fall short:

. . . .
And all men in their praying, self-deceived, address
The coinage of their own unquiet thoughts, unless

Thou in magnetic mercy to Thyself divert
Our arrows, aimed unskillfully, beyond desert;
And all men are idolaters, crying unheard
To a deaf idol, if Thou take them at their word.

Take not, O Lord, our literal sense. Lord, in thy great
Unbroken speech our limping metaphor translate.[10]

Lewis reminds us here that we do not and cannot tell "the whole truth," even in prayer, as that can only be spoken in the one, original Word, toward whom our language and symbols and images direct us, through a glass darkly.

The words we find and use in prayer are a reaching toward God, who must reach down from humanly unbridgeable heights to receive them. But we have been told and taught to pray, and so our work in prayer is to make our words an offering and let God make them worthy.

10. C. S. Lewis, "Footnote to All Prayers," in *Poems* (New York: Harvest Books, 2002), p. 131.

Cherish Silence

A friend of mine who worked in the corporate head-
quarters of a large company told me about a colleague's protest against the grating Muzak one was
forced to hear while waiting, on hold, for an in-house
phone connection. After some deliberation, the powers
that be decided to make due accommodation. Soon
thereafter, when one was put on hold, a voice message
assured the listener, "You are being put on hold. Your
party will answer your call as soon as possible. In the
meantime, silence will be provided." What a gift to the
corporate world! I wonder if some workers might not
have called in just to hear some of the silence "provided"
on particularly busy days.

Silence is hard to come by, especially in urban life. Indeed, the practice of silence has had to become more and
more deliberate as we surround ourselves with ubiquitous means of filling or simply obliterating it: car radios,
iPods, background music in restaurants, constantly pro-
liferating ways of being tuned in and hooked up that pro-

tect us from silences that can seem so threatening. Noise insulates us from the silence that exposes us to encounters with self and God, and to the voice of the Spirit that groans within us in ways we may not control. To choose silence is to risk that encounter. But if we are to care for the work that words do, we must be willing to open up silences in our minds and our days. Our words matter only to the extent that they have been allowed to germinate and take root in silence.

Since germination suggests the biblical metaphor of the seed, let us pursue that metaphor for a moment. In the practice of *lectio divina,* you are directed to read short passages of Scripture repeatedly, listening for the word or phrase that addresses you in a particular way in the moment. Once you are led to pause over a particular word or phrase, you take time to hear it — simply to hear it, without analysis or exegesis or any other rational process. You let it fall into your mind and heart like a seed falling into prepared soil. There, like the seed, the word begins its work. In the silence, gradually, the word begins to yield associations, images, feelings, sometimes whole sentences, that provide what is needful for the moment. What is yielded may not be usable or seem relevant at once, but if it is faithfully received and noted, some understanding may come that would have been impossible without having received the word in the context of contemplative silence. The last of four slow readings recommended in this practice is simply to "rest in the word":

224

having received it, allowed it to yield what it may yield, the reader simply dwells in the echo of intimate utterance, letting the word sink to the place where "deep calls unto deep."

The silence we practice is one fairly reliable measure of the distance between effective words and ineffectual babble. We encourage glibness by incessant focus on productivity and by the utilitarian idea that time, space, and the airwaves must be "filled." We churn out reports and memos, meet and discuss and debate and assess and strategize in schools and corporations and even in churches without generally making explicit the need for silent reflection as a vital part of those processes. Even so-called retreat weekends — when colleagues gather apart from the workplace, take off their ties or nylons, don their jeans, and head for the woods — are often more like brainstorming sessions or extended business meetings. The skill and clarity and trust it takes actually to choose and cultivate corporate silence is rare. In a culture that practices it so little — in which, like fallow soil, it is often misperceived as a wasted resource that could be expropriated for profit — we hardly know what to do with it. And so our conversation suffers in the same way that our crops suffer from exhausted soil that has been allowed no time for replenishment.

Very little in our culture teaches or encourages us to rest in this way. The rhythms of speaking and keeping

225

still, working and resting, engaging and withdrawing, are so deeply disrupted that even the concept of Sabbath, even for the pious, is hard to retrieve. The old agricultural principle of allowing ground to remain fallow to give the soil time to renew itself is regularly violated by "agribusinesses" so intent upon short-term productivity that they inject dying soil with artificial fertilizers, achieving a lengthened utility with diminished quality — similar to the ways in which end-of-life technologies can prolong dying and call it living. Renewal time, whether for the soil or for relationship or for interior life — the time when we stop, let be, withdraw, do nothing, say nothing — is too frequently redefined as a wasted asset. So we live impoverished, deprived of the day that enriches the rest of the week or the silence that frames and illuminates our reading and our speech.

To stay with the image of germination, let us also consider the time it takes for words to come to fruition. During thirty years of teaching I have been privileged to witness this process repeatedly in conversations with students who, having read a passage from the work at hand, underlined it, discussed it in class, written papers about it, and sometimes gone on to graduation and beyond, arrive at a moment of delayed epiphany when that particular text turns out to be precisely the instrument of understanding they need in a situation they couldn't have foreseen. Suddenly a line from Dante or Dostoyevsky will deliver its wisdom just, it seems, in due time.

To shift the metaphor slightly, we might consider how silence is like water — cleansing, opening what is closed, slaking elemental thirst. Silence is to words what water is to the body and to the earth. Words, like food, nourish and support life in ways that reach beyond metaphor to solid fact. But it is in our silences that digestive and regenerative processes can take place. Pauses in conversation in which one puffs on a pipe, gazes off toward the horizon, or putters allow one to "chew on" what has been said, to consider whether one can "swallow" or "stomach" it, to "take it in." All the language in the Psalms about tasting and eating the word invokes this rich metaphor. We taste words like honey in our mouths or like meat and drink; but it is in the silences of the interior — body and soul — where the regenerative processes take place, beneath the reach of our conscious control.

Or again, we might consider silence as a place we enter. Like the sacred spaces we design for retreat and worship, silence offers us a sanctuary from the clatter of the world that is too much with us. There something is protected and sheltered so as to recover from the buffetings of noise and haste. In the hospitality of our own silences and of others', we receive the hospice care we need to claim life in the midst of death. There words may be sifted, guarded, nourished, and held until they begin to yield what we need. We need literal places of silence in order to open up the interior "places" of silence that allow us to ponder, consider, contemplate, reflect, and receive what we need. Silence as a spiritual discipline and practice can hardly be cultivated without the walk in the woods, the open chapel, the "room of one's own" that guard us from intrusion. Once we are there, silence may begin to become a state of mind and heart. In the quiet interior, conversation with self and God may take place that begins with the hearing of the "still, small voice." There, as Eliot puts it, "words, after speech, reach/into the silence."[1] Lifted out of the babble that surrounds them, they yield unforeseen gifts and are revitalized as instruments of understanding. As Bonhoeffer notes, "Meditation is not having great thoughts, but loving the words you hear and letting them shape you."[2] Such silence is neither mute nor empty, but rich and full.

We may go for days, sometimes for months, without such a practice, but eventually we begin to hear our own words as blather. Without silence, language becomes noise. It might seem a reliable measure of our need for silence simply to pay attention to the feeling Wordsworth articulated so memorably in his declaration that "the world is too much with us" — I might even say within us — but I think sometimes we have so raised our tolerance for babble that it is harder to detect the need for silence

1. T. S. Eliot, *Burnt Norton,* in *The Complete Poems and Plays of T. S. Eliot* (New York: Harcourt, Brace & World, 1971).

2. Dietrich Bonhoeffer, *The Way to Freedom, 1935-1939,* in *The Collected Works of Dietrich Bonhoeffer* (San Francisco: Harper & Row, 1966), pp. 59-61.

than it may once have been. Background noise is not only a fact of life but an addiction. I speak from my own experience here. The first few days of any vacation seem to me to require adaptation to the loss of the very stimuli and sounds I complain about. Where there is no cell-phone reception, radio, or wireless access, I have to be weaned once again from dependencies I both resent and cling to.

On a recent stay in rural Scotland, I had occasion to reflect on the humbling fact that for most of history, people had no concept of or capacity to "stay in touch" as we now routinely expect. "Good-bye" — "God be with you" — was often literally a prayer of letting go, perhaps unto death. Long voyages with no phones and intermittent, unreliable postal service, and before that, widespread illiteracy, put a much higher price on parting. Before you went on your way, you commended your loved ones to God. Glad as I am for my daughter's voice on the phone, or a grandchild's, I do wonder how to assess the price we pay for all our staying in touch. Certainly we pay far less attention to those immediately around us; real presence gives way to the selective, electronically mediated contacts of our choosing. Those who cross our paths, who may have unexpected gifts for us, are much more likely to be ignored. And as we get older, the Christmas list lengthens, the number of former students, colleagues, club and church members who seem to have some claim on us expands to a point where deep and focused conversation with those given to us in the present may be dissipated in much superficial communicating. We say more and more about less and less to more and more people. E-mail and Facebook multiplied this problem exponentially. We have traded deep, sustained, intimate conversation for vast and sometimes overwhelming forms and means of "communication."

So how are we to live rightly with words? How do we retrieve from the increased babble in print and on airwaves the words we need as equipment for living? The old Jewish practice of binding a text from holy writ to a child's wrist as he was sent out for the day offers a literal example of a kind of trust in the power of the word to equip and enable us that we might do well to retrieve. To come to the one who "has the words of eternal life" and to hear them is not necessarily to act on or even understand them at once, but, like Mary, to "ponder them" — literally, to bear the weight of them — in our hearts until the moment comes for them to flower into understanding. The place of inner silence is where they are carried. To cherish words is necessarily to cherish the silence into which they enter and upon which they depend. Elie Wiesel's rich formation in Judaism gave him life-saving reliance on the words of the Torah. He testifies to the importance of the silences that allow words their resonance in reflecting on the secular discourses that have made it harder to "hear" the word: "Today other books [than the Torah] hold me in their grip, and I try to learn from other storytellers how to pierce the meaning of an experience. . . . But most of them talk too much. Their song is lost in words, like rivers in the sand."[3] The "song" he speaks of is that core or thread of loving wisdom that is the kernel of meaning in any utterance worth the breath of life that bears it.

We are not without models of silence as spiritual practice. Monasteries, both hermitages where silence is a way of life and those that simply observe periods of silence through the day and the "great silence" at night, still offer their extraordinary hospitality to the world-weary. Quakers still gather weekly on "first day" in corporate silence to listen for the Spirit, each speaking, if at all, only once and briefly to drop words into the silence as a free gift to whomever they might serve. An encouraging number of "intentional" communities or households committed to spiritual survival by countercultural means include shared periods of silence as part of their rhythm of life together. Elizabeth O'Connor, writing about such a community in Washington, D.C., describes such silence as a form of fasting — "the practice, on one day a week, of speaking only when it was essential, and then to use the minimum of words necessary for communication." Such exercises were designed, she explains, "to help us find our own center, and then to act and speak out of that place of quiet." And she goes on to report the result of this

3. Elie Wiesel, *Legends of Our Time* (New York: Schocken Books, reprint edition, 2004).

practice: "When we begin to hear through our opaque and clumsy words what our own beings utter, then perhaps we will begin to hear what someone else is struggling to say. That is how communion begins."[4]

If such practices seem spiritually and practically unattainable for those of us who don't inhabit monasteries or intentional communities, but rather two-career households with sundry children, houseguests, and suburban distractions, I pass along the amusing advice I received from a dear mentor years ago. Speaking of the need for quiet reflection before responding to others' requests or pleas for our time and attention, she suggested that even so small a thing as a retreat to the bathroom before offering an answer might provide the time necessary for silent listening for inner guidance. To cultivate and cherish silence is sometimes that simple. The short pauses in between encounters are often all it takes to give them depth and deliberation, and to find the needful words.

In a somewhat sharper vein, Thoreau needles readers of *Walden* into reconsidering the costs of sociability:

> If we would enjoy the most intimate society with that in each of us which is without, or above, being spoken to, we must not only be silent, but commonly so far

4. Elizabeth O'Connor, *The Search for Silence* (Waco, Tex.: Word Books, 1972), pp. 97, 125, 21.

apart bodily that we cannot possibly hear each other's voice in any case. Referred to this standard, speech is for the convenience of those who are hard of hearing; but there are many fine things which we cannot say if we have to shout.[5]

Somewhat whimsically, but provocatively, Thoreau suggests here not only how silence may be necessary to provide the acoustical space in which the effects of words may be adequately felt, but also how much of what we call communion takes place beneath or beyond the range of words.

Poets know this. They cannot do their work without silence. One of the distinguishing features of poetry is the way it makes silences explicit. Line breaks that leave a wide white margin prose might have filled, stanza breaks that sometimes come startlingly in the midst of an unfinished sentence, all the white space that meets the reader's eye — these betoken the ambient silence in which the poem does its work. In *Ash Wednesday,* T. S. Eliot asks, "Where shall the word be found, where will the word/Resound? Not here, there is not enough silence."[6]

Samuel Beckett brought a practical understanding of Eliot's claim to bear in the direction of his own plays. He

5. Henry David Thoreau, *Walden; Or, Life in the Woods* (Mineola, N.Y.: Dover Publishers, Thrift Edition, 1995), p. 167.
6. T. S. Eliot, *Ash Wednesday,* in *The Complete Poems and Plays of T. S. Eliot,* p. 65.

gave actors meticulous instructions about making sure the silences and pauses had their due. He prescribed a particular number of seconds for "pause" and more seconds for "silence" partly to push the audience's tolerance for and awareness of shared silence. Just a few seconds was enough to challenge the comfort levels of most audiences.[7]

We need that challenge, and the best of our artists offer it, finding inventive ways to open up and clear interior spaces, weaving words around what cannot be said, ringing the silences we avoid with chant, plainsong, the ding of a Tibetan chime, giving shape to the silence so that we may recognize it not as void or abyss but as a place to lie down in green pastures and be restored.

They trace paths for us to the threshold of unspeakable mystery. There we lay down our pens and swords, and the rest is silence. Silence is the Sabbath we need. In silence we take our rest.

7. See Samuel Beckett, *Theatrical Notebooks of Samuel Beckett: Waiting for Godot* (New York: Grove Press, reprint edition, 1994).

Bibliography

Appleton, George, ed. *The Oxford Book of Prayer.* New York: Oxford University Press, 1985.

Appolinaire, Guillaume. *Alcools.* Paris: Klincksieck, 1997.

Austen, Jane. *Pride and Prejudice.* 1813; New York: Random House (Bantam Dell edition), 2003.

Bachelard, Gaston. *The Poetics of Space.* Trans. Maria Jolas. Boston: Beacon Press, 1964.

Beckett, Samuel. *Theatrical Notebooks of Samuel Beckett: Waiting for Godot.* New York: Grove Press, reprint edition, 1994.

Berry, Wendell. *Collected Poems of Wendell Berry, 1957-1982.* San Francisco: North Point Press, 1987.

————. "Making It Home." In *Fidelity: Five Stories.* New York: Pantheon Books, 1993.

————. "Standing by Words." In *Standing by Words.* Washington, D.C.: Shoemaker & Hoard, reprint edition, 2005.

Bettelheim, Bruno. *The Uses of Enchantment: The Meaning and Importance of Fairy Tales.* East Sussex, U.K.: Gardners Books, 1991.

Bloch, Chana, and Ariel Bloch, trans. *The Song of Songs.* Berkeley and Los Angeles: University of California Press, 1998.

Bonhoeffer, Dietrich. *The Way to Freedom, 1935-1939.* In *The Collected Works of Dietrich Bonhoeffer.* San Francisco: Harper & Row (1st U.S. edition), 1966.

Bryson, Bill. *Made in America: An Informal History of the English Language in the United States.* New York: Harper Perennial, 1994.

Chesterton, G. K. *Orthodoxy.* San Francisco: Ignatius Press, reprint edition, 1995.

———. *What's Wrong with the World.* In *New World Chesterton.* New York: Sheed & Ward, 1956.

Ciardi, John, and Miller Williams. *How Does a Poem Mean?* Boston: Houghton Mifflin, 1960.

Collins, Billy. ed. *Poetry 180: A Turning Back to Poetry.* New York: Random House, 2003.

E. E. Cummings. *E. E. Cummings: Complete Poems, 1914-1962,* ed. George J. Firmage (New York: Liveright, 1991), p. 291.

———. *Six Nonlectures.* Cambridge: Harvard University Press, reprint, 1991.

Daniell, David. *The Bible in English: Its History and Influence.* New Haven: Yale University Press, 2003.

Davis, Garrick. "Reading at Risk." NEA Newsroom, 8 July 2004, available at www.nea.gov/news/news04/ReadingAtRisk.html.

Dickinson, Emily. *Complete Poems of Emily Dickinson,* ed. Thomas Johnson. Boston: Little, Brown & Co., 1960.

Dillard, Annie. *Pilgrim at Tinker Creek.* New York: Harper & Row, 1974, Perennial Classics edition, 1998.

Donne, John. *The Complete Poetry and Selected Prose of John Donne.* New York: Random House, Modern Library, 1952.

Dostoyevsky, Fyodor. *Notes from Underground.* New York: Vintage Books, reprint edition, 1994.

Eliot, T. S. *The Complete Poems and Plays of T. S. Eliot.* New York: Harcourt, Brace & World, 1971.

Faulkner, William. *Absalom, Absalom!* New York: Modern Library, The Corrected Text, 1993.

Forster, E. M. *Aspects of the Novel.* London: Edward Arnold, Publishers, Abinger edition, 1974.

Bibliography

Fowles, John. *Daniel Martin.* Boston: Back Bay Books, reprint edition, 1987.

Franken, Al. *Lies and the Lying Liars Who Tell Them.* New York: Penguin Books, 2003.

Frost, Robert. *The Poetry of Robert Frost.* New York: Holt, Rinehart & Winston, 1969.

Hardy, Thomas. *Thomas Hardy: The Complete Poems.* Ed. James Gibson. London: Macmillan & Co., 2002.

Hass, Robert, ed. *The Essential Haiku: Versions of Basho, Buson, and Issa.* Hopewell, N.J.: Ecco Press, 1994.

Hawthorne, Nathaniel. *The Scarlet Letter.* New York: Vintage Books, Library of America edition, 1990.

Hesse, Hermann. *Steppenwolf.* New York: Picador, reprint edition, 2002.

Hirsch, E. D. *Cultural Literacy: What Every American Needs to Know.* New York: Vintage Books, 1988.

Hopkins, Gerard Manley. *Poems and Prose of Gerard Manley Hopkins.* Ed. W. H. Gardner. Baltimore: Penguin Books, 1961.

James, Henry. *The Ambassadors.* New York: W. W. Norton, 2d edition, 1994.

Lamott, Anne. *Traveling Mercies: Some Thoughts on Faith.* New York: Random House, 2000.

Lao Tse. *Tao Te Ching.* Trans. Jonathan Star. Los Angeles: Jeremy Tarcher, 2001.

LeGuin, Ursula. "The Ones Who Walk Away from Omelas." In *The Wind's Twelve Quarters.* New York: Harper & Row, 1975.

Lewis, C. S. *Poems.* New York: Harvest Books, 2002.

Luguri, James. *To Make a World: One Hundred Haiku and One Waka.* Peter Luguri, 1987.

McEntyre, Marilyn, ed. *Word Tastings.* Santa Barbara: Santa Barbara Review Publications, 1998.

McKibben, Bill. *Hundred-Dollar Holiday: The Case for a More Joyful Christmas.* New York: Simon & Schuster, 1998.

McWhorter, John. *Doing Our Own Thing: The Degradation of Language and Music and Why We Should, Like, Care.* New York: Gotham, reprint edition, 2004.

Mohrmann, Margaret. *Medicine as Ministry.* Cleveland: Pilgrim Press, 1995.

Muggeridge, Malcolm. *Something Beautiful for God.* San Francisco: Harper, 1986.

Nachmanovitch, Stephen. *Free Play: Improvisation in Life and Art.* Los Angeles: Jeremy Tarcher, 1990.

Nemerov, Howard. "Bottom's Dream: The Likeness of Poems and Jokes." In *Reflections on Poetry and Poetics.* New Brunswick, N.J.: Rutgers University Press, 1972.

O'Connor, Elizabeth. *The Search for Silence.* Waco, Tex.: Word Books, 1972.

O'Connor, Flannery. *Mystery and Manners.* New York: Farrar, Straus & Giroux, 1969.

Oliver, Mary. *New and Selected Poems.* Boston: Beacon Press, 1992.

Olson, Theodore. *Hawk's Way.* The League to Support Poetry, 1941.

Orwell, George. *1984.* New York: Penguin Books/Plume, reissue edition, 1983.

————. "Politics and the English Language." In *George Orwell: A Collection of Essays.* New York: Harcourt, 1946; Harvest edition, 1981.

Ozick, Cynthia. *Metaphor and Memory.* New York: Vintage Books, reprint edition, 1991.

Pascal, Blaise. *Pensées.* Trans. A. J. Krailsheimer. New York: Penguin Classics, reissue edition, 1995.

Pieper, Josef. *Leisure: The Basis of Culture.* Review online: www.newjerusalem.com/pieper.htm.

Polti, Georges. *The Thirty-Six Dramatic Situations.* New York: Writer, 1977. See also http://www.rpglibrary.org/articles/storytelling/36plots.html.

Pound, Ezra. "Vorticism." In *Gaudier-Brzeska: A Memoir.* New York: New Directions, 1970.

Bibliography

Quammen, David. "The Troubled Gaze of the Octopus." In *Natural Acts: A Sidelong View of Science and Nature.* New York: Avon Books, 1996.

Refuel: The Complete New Testament. Nashville: Thomas Nelson, Inc., 2003.

Revolve: The Complete New Testament. Nashville: Thomas Nelson, Inc., 2003.

Rilke, Rainer Maria. *The Selected Poetry of Rainer Maria Rilke.* Ed. and trans. Stephen Mitchell. New York: Vintage Books, 1989.

Robinson, Marilynne. *Housekeeping.* New York: Picador, reprint edition, 2004.

Rodenburg, Patsy. *The Need for Words.* New York: Theater Arts Books, 1993.

Sacks, Oliver. "The Man Who Mistook His Wife for a Hat." In *The Man Who Mistook His Wife for a Hat and Other Clinical Tales.* New York: Simon & Schuster/Touchstone, 1998.

Sanders, Barry. *A Is for Ox.* New York: Pantheon Books, 1994.

Shakespeare, William. *William Shakespeare: The Sonnets.* Ed. Douglas Bush and Alfred Harbage. New York: Penguin Books, reprint, 1977.

Sider, Ron. *Rich Christians in an Age of Hunger.* Nashville: W. Publishing Group, 1997.

Smith, Ken. *Junk English.* New York: Blast Books, 2001.

Steiner, George. *Language and Silence: Essays on Language, Literature, and the Inhuman.* New York: Atheneum, 1958, 1982.

———. *No Passion Spent.* New Haven: Yale University Press, 1996.

———. *Real Presences.* Chicago: University of Chicago Press, reprint edition, 1991.

Stevens, Wallace. *The Collected Poems of Wallace Stevens.* New York: Vintage Books, reissue edition, 1990.

———. *The Palm at the End of the Mind: Selected Poems and a Play.* Ed. Holly Stevens. New York: Vintage Books, 1971.

Storm, Hyemeyohsts. *Seven Arrows.* New York: Ballantine Books, 1972.

Taylor, Edward. *The Poems of Edward Taylor.* Ed. Donald E. Stanford. Chapel Hill: University of North Carolina Press, 1989.

Thoreau, Henry David. *Walden; Or, Life in the Woods.* Mineola, N.Y.: Dover Publishers, Thrift edition, 1995.

Tripp, Diane Karay, ed. *Prayers from the Reformed Tradition: In the Company of a Great Cloud of Witnesses.* Louisville: Witherspoon Press, 2001.

Twain, Mark. "Fenimore Cooper's Literary Offenses." In *The Unabridged Mark Twain,* ed. Lawrence Teacher. Philadelphia: Running Press, 1976.

Van Doren, Mark. *Collected Poems, 1922-1938.* New York: Henry Holt & Co., 1939.

Weaver, Paul. *News and the Culture of Lying.* New York: Free Press, 1994.

Wiesel, Elie. *Legends of Our Time.* New York: Schocken Books, reprint edition, 2004.

Wilbur, Richard. *Richard Wilbur: New and Collected Poems.* New York: Harcourt Brace Jovanovich, 1988.

Williams, William Carlos. *The Collected Poems of William Carlos Williams, Volume 2: 1939-1962.* New York: New Directions Publishing, reprint, 1991.

Yeats, W. B. *Collected Poems of W. B. Yeats.* 2d rev. ed. New York: Scribner, 1996.

Acknowledgments

The author and publisher gratefully acknowledge permission to quote the following material:

Excerpts from "There's a certain slant of light" and "Tell all the truth, but tell it slant" by Emily Dickinson. Reprinted by permission of the publishers and the Trustees of Amherst College from *The Poems of Emily Dickinson,* ed. Thomas H. Johnson. Cambridge, Mass.: The Belknap Press of Harvard University Press. Copyright © 1951, 1955, 1979, 1983 by the President and Fellows of Harvard College.

Two haiku from James Luguri's *To Make a World: One Hundred Haiku and One Waka,* privately published in Berkeley, California. Reprinted by permission of Peter Luguri.

The poem "Hawk" by Mary Oliver. Reprinted by permission of Beacon Press from *New and Selected Poems* by Mary Oliver. Boston: Beacon Press, 1992.

Excerpt from "The Eye" by Richard Wilbur, copyright © 1975 by Richard Wilbur. From *The Mind-Reader* by Richard Wilbur. New York: Harcourt Brace, 1976. Reprinted by permission of Houghton Mifflin Harcourt Publishing Company.

The prayer "God of Mercy and of Grace." Reprinted by permission of St. Andrew Press. From *The Book of Common Order of the Church of Scotland,* 1994 edition, and reprinted in *Prayers from the Reformed Tradition,* ed. Diane Karay Tripp. Louisville: Witherspoon Press, 2001.

Excerpt from "Footnote to All Prayers" from *Poems* by C.S. Lewis. Copyright © 1964 by the Executors of the Estate of C.S. Lewis and renewed 1992 by C.S. Lewis Pte. Ltd. Reprinted by permission of Houghton Mifflin Harcourt Publishing Company.